PRAISE FOR HEIDI KÜHN AND
BREAKING GROUND

"Guided by the leadership of Heidi Kühn, Roots of Peace has saved lives, transformed communities, and advanced peace around the globe. Long after the bombs have been silenced and the peace treaties have been signed, the deadly threat of landmines remains. We must maintain our drumbeat of activism and action until every child and parent can live free from the senseless devastation caused by landmines. Thank you Heidi Kühn, for your work healing war-torn communities by turning these fields into productive farmland to grow and sell crops on the global market. Your steadfast dedication to securing peace and ensuring economic empowerment for so many is critical and greatly appreciated."

—NANCY PELOSI
Speaker of the US House of Representatives

"There are an estimated sixty million landmines in over sixty countries, [the] aftermath of civil wars. They maim or kill farmers and children. They also cause terrible harm to animals, domestic livestock and wildlife alike. . . . Thank you, Heidi Kuhn, for writing *Breaking Ground*, [which] discusses this mostly forgotten aspect."

—JANE GOODALL, PhD, DBE
Founder, the Jane Goodall Institute, and UN Messenger of Peace

"[Heidi Kühn has] turned mines into vines by replacing the seeds of destruction with the seeds of life . . . and [she has] shown the world that, even with modest beginnings, a partnership backed up by persistence can make a real difference."

—THE LATE KOFI ANNAN
Former United Nations Secretary-General and Nobel Peace Prize laureate

"In Heidi Kühn's new book, *Breaking Ground*, the power of humanity and good over evil is clear as a bell. This is Heidi's extraordinary journey of planting grapevines where there were once landmines, and hope where there was once despair. Heidi is a woman who has put her life on the line for peace, justice, and renewal—echoes of the work that was done by Princess Diana as well as thousands of others in the fight against terror toward children and other living things in the struggle to eliminate landmines around the world. Heidi is my hero and will be yours when you read her new amazing book."

—JUDY COLLINS
Singer, songwriter, and activist

"I have walked through minefields with Heidi Kühn in Afghanistan, Vietnam, and the Middle East. I covered the stories of the nonprofit she founded for more than fifteen years as a news anchor. . . . Heidi Kühn is an extraordinary visionary who is following her dream to stop landmine violence around the world. Her courage is undeniable [and her] commitment is unstoppable, as Roots of Peace replaces landmines with grapevines or pepper vines or fruit trees in war-ravaged nations. . . . I was a witness to highly successful efforts in Afghanistan and Vietnam, where sustainable agricultural production is working to bring economic prosperity. Please read this book. It may inspire you to believe in your own dreams of making positive changes in our world."

—CHERYL JENNINGS
Emmy Award-winning journalist

"As her memoir documents, Heidi's own walks through minefields were the beginning of a much longer journey, one inspired by her determination to transform a history of fear and tragedy into a story of hope and triumph. Her determined pursuit of her vision of turning mines into vines has spared thousands of real people from death and disfiguration, while giving them new livelihoods and new hope. *Breaking Ground* is a testament to Heidi's faith and raw courage and to her persistence in the face of seemingly impossible odds. It is an affirmation of the human capacity to do good in the world, one that could not be more welcome or more timely."

—AMBASSADOR GEORGE MOOSE
Vice Chair, U.S. Institute of Peace

"More than a dozen United Nations entities play a role in mine-action programs around the world. But much of the actual work is carried out by courageous and stalwart nongovernmental organizations like Roots of Peace. Together, in recent years, we have cleared tens of millions of square meters of land, destroyed hundreds of thousands of mines, . . . and educated millions of people about mine issues. Behind these numbers are moving stories of limbs spared, lives saved, and anguish avoided. . . . Mine action does more than avert suffering; it lays the foundation for development and peace. Roads once unusable fill with traffic; land once laid to waste sprouts with hospitals and homes, schools, and crops. This is tangible, meaningful progress. I commend Roots of Peace for its leadership in international efforts to replace the detritus of war with the fruits of peace."

—BAN KI-MOON
Former United Nations Secretary-General

"Heidi Kühn embodies the notion that one person can make a difference, can change lives, and [can] save lives. . . . Roots of Peace has helped clear land, fund training for deminers in that dangerous work, and discover what plants—grapes, pepper, nuts, other fruits— can thrive in that soil. She has built partnerships here and abroad, made countless trips to the front lines, raised millions to underwrite the cause, helped wounded survivors, and saved countless others.

Breaking Ground tells this compelling and moving story. Heidi Kühn is an inspiration to us all."

—GILLIAN SORENSEN
Former United Nations Assistant Secretary-General for External Relations

"From her days as a producer reporting for CNN in the Soviet Union to surviving cancer and ultimately pioneering a new path to remove landmines and heal the wounds of war, Heidi Kühn has taken a dangerous path towards peace . . . quite literally replacing the dangers of landmines with roots for vines. In her new book *Breaking Ground*, she inspires us to do our part, to get engaged, and [to] support innovative solutions that plant the seeds for future prosperity and peace."

—PAT MITCHELL
*First woman CEO of PBS, current chair of the Sundance Institute, and author
of* Becoming a Dangerous Woman: Embracing Risk to Change the World

"Prepare to be amazed and inspired! Heidi Kühn weaves a tale of motherhood, empathy, and empowerment. Her belief is powerful—belief in God, belief in the goodness of communities everywhere, and absolute belief that she could make a global difference."

—MAJOR GENERAL BARBARA J. FAULKENBERRY
US Air Force

"I was injured by a landline in Israel when I was eleven years old. Immediately after my injury I was determined to take action. I didn't want anybody else to suffer like I did. Fortunately, I was approached by the amazing people of Roots of Peace. Together, we [drafted] a historic humanitarian law to remove all landmines in Israel. . . . That's when I met Heidi. She inspired me never to give up. . . . You will love her book *Breaking Ground*, as it is a true story of seeking peaceful solutions in our one world!"

—DANIEL YUVAL
Landmine survivor, Israel

"It was horrifying to see my husband, Guy, carry my son, who was missing a leg, as bloodshed shattered our lives. Almost immediately, Heidi Kühn connected with us and helped us to rehabilitate as a family. Working with my son, Daniel, [Roots of Peace] helped to bring forth the historic [Minefield Clearance Act] in March 2011. As a mother, I hope that *Breaking Ground* will be translated into many languages, as landmines know no borders!"

—TALI YUVAL
Mother of landmine survivor Daniel Yuval, Israel

"*Breaking Ground* is an elegant and insightful look into [Heidi Kühn's] story and vision of making a difference in war-torn lands—a truly remarkable approach of removing, restoring, and rebuilding that has and will continue to make a huge impact on future generations to come, not only in Afghanistan but all over the world. Heidi's passion and dedication to this mission [are] truly inspirational; it is a powerful and deeply personal story that the world needs to hear. . . . We talk about changing the hearts and minds to win the fight—her actions have changed not only the hearts and minds but the outlook for a better life for so many."

—GENERAL JOHN F. CAMPBELL
US Army

"Heidi's passion for advancing peace through the elimination of landmines has been evident since I first met her in 1997. As a survivor of war, I know firsthand its awful results and have supported her vision to turn mines to vines, starting in my homeland of Croatia. Her story will inform and move you."

—MILJENKO "MIKE" GRGICH
Founder and CEO of Grgich Hills Estate, Napa Valley, California

"Heidi Kühn is a force. The energy, dedication, and purity of mission she expresses in her personal life is matched only by her focus to eradicate landmines across the globe. Her book, *Breaking Ground*, documents the challenges she has experienced in her own life and how she has transformed her own hardships into inspirational teachings that children and adults can understand and use to improve their own lives. How Heidi touches people around the world is spiritual, practical, and symbolic, as she leads the effort to rid the world of landmines and literally plants seeds for a future that will be safer and more prosperous for generations."

—JOHN F. DUNBAR
Mayor of Yountville, California

"[Heidi Kühn's] work of uniting people across the world by eliminating landmines and replacing them with food, spices, and flowers is fantastic—an achievement that deserves to be supported and recognized."

—CLAES NOBEL
President, United Earth

"[Heidi Kühn] is driven by a compassionate humanitarian impulse to rid the world of . . . threats to innocent civilians and especially children. [She] has been living this theme through her Roots of Peace organization in those parts of the world still beset with these long-lasting killers."

—KENNETH M. QUINN
*President of the World Food Prize Foundation and former
US Ambassador to the Kingdom of Cambodia*

BREAKING GROUND

FROM LANDMINES TO GRAPEVINES,
ONE WOMAN'S MISSION TO
HEAL THE WORLD

BREAKING GROUND

FROM LANDMINES TO GRAPEVINES, ONE WOMAN'S MISSION TO HEAL THE WORLD

HEIDI KÜHN

Foreword by Her Majesty Queen Noor
Preface by Dr. Ken Rutherford

EARTH AWARE

SAN RAFAEL · LOS ANGELES · LONDON

EARTH AWARE

An Imprint of MandalaEarth
PO Box 3088
San Rafael, CA 94912
www.MandalaEarth.com

Find us on Facebook: www.facebook.com/MandalaEarth
Follow us on Twitter: @MandalaEarth

Library of Congress Cataloging-in-Publication Data available.

ISBN: 978-1-68383-446-5

Publisher: Raoul Goff
President: Kate Jerome
Associate Publisher: Phillip Jones
Creative Director: Chrissy Kwasnik
VP of Manufacturing: Alix Nicholaeff
Designer: Malea Clark-Nicholson
Managing Editor: Lauren LePera
Senior Production Editor: Rachel Anderson
Senior Production Manager: Greg Steffen

Cover images courtesy of Phan Tan Lam (top) and Hamid
Ansary (bottom). Author photo courtesy of Cheryl Jennings.
All other images courtesy of Roots of Peace.

ROOTS of PEACE   ⊕ REPLANTED PAPER

Earth Aware Editions, in association with Roots of Peace,
will plant two trees for each tree used in the manufacturing
of this book. Roots of Peace is an internationally renowned
humanitarian organization dedicated to eradicating land mines
worldwide and converting war-torn lands into productive farms
and wildlife habitats. Roots of Peace will plant two million fruit
and nut trees in Afghanistan and provide farmers there with the
skills and support necessary for sustainable land use.

Manufactured in India by Insight Editions
10 9 8 7 6 5 4 3 2 1

CONTENTS

This book is dedicated to
my beloved husband, Gary,
my partner in life and
in the work of Roots of Peace;

to our four wonderful children,
Brooks, Tucker, Kyleigh, and Christian,
who have walked this path
with their parents and with full hearts;

to my dad,
for giving me the gift of life and
instilling in me the California pioneer
spirit to believe in myself;

and to my mother,
for teaching me forgiveness.

FOREWORD

Her Majesty Queen Noor

For over forty years of my life and work in the Middle East, I have personally witnessed the unique threat posed by antipersonnel landmines to civilians, entire communities, and developmental progress, because as "weapons of mass destruction in slow motion," they continue destroying lives and livestock and holding valuable agricultural land hostage long after conflict has stopped. They are a modern man-made epidemic.

In the modern Holy Land, if Jesus were to have spent his forty days in the wilderness, or if Elijah were to have crossed the River Jordan, or if John the Baptist were to have proclaimed his message of repentance, they would have had to survive not only the ancient tests of hunger and thirst but the modern threat of minefields.

Even as recently as twenty years ago, in spite of our army's diligent clearance of hundreds of thousands of mines in the Jordan Valley, when I planned to visit near the site where John the Baptist preached and baptized, I was confined to restricted pathways through the not-yet-completely-demined surrounding region's stark but beautiful wilderness. I was struck by the sad irony of this in one of the world's most spiritually significant landscapes, revered by Jews, Christians, and Muslims, where prophets like Moses and companions of the Prophet Muhammad had preached. The Prophet Muhammad PBUH said, "*imatatu al-'atha 'an al-tareeq sadaqah*": "The removal of things that cause suffering from the path is a good deed." What was once a metaphorical moral precept has become a literal necessity—a prophecy too true for comfort.

Since 2012, clearance of the known minefields in the Jordan Valley has been completed; this ground, which is holy for billions around the world, is no longer desecrated by mines, and pilgrims who wish to walk on the paths of the prophets can do so in safety.

However, all too many post-conflict regions have not been so fortunate. When peace is declared, the guns and mortars are stilled, but no one turns off the mines. And because they are small and destroy lives one by one, their horrific and heartbreaking consequences can go as unnoticed as the mines themselves.

I have seen firsthand the devastation caused by loss of life, limb, and livelihood to individuals, families, and entire communities; not only in rural Jordan and other countries in our region but also—through my work with the Landmine Survivors Network and the International Campaign to Ban Landmines—among those striving to overcome the wreckage landmines have wrought on their lives and future prospects in Africa, Cambodia, Vietnam, the Balkans, the United States, and Europe.

Survivors of conflict are fighting to overcome many different traumas—from the physical effects of bombs and bullets to the psychological devastation caused by hatred and loss to the economic havoc, political instability, and social unrest that follow in the wake of war. Their needs range from immediate medical assistance to rehabilitation, from help with returning home to economic assistance and training, from help with rebuilding private livelihoods and public infrastructures to help with learning once again to live in peace.

But for survivors to recover, communities also need to recover. Recovery from major trauma is harrowing under the best of circumstances and with the best of care. Recovery in the absence of the most basic necessities of life—adequate food, medication, housing, and social support—is a miracle. In the aftermath of conflict, communities often face a complex of problems: damaged infrastructure and public services, poverty and unemployment, a degraded environment, precious agricultural land held hostage by landmines and unexploded ordnances (UXOs), and the proliferation of small arms.

Immense effort and resources are spent reacting to the immediate humanitarian emergencies that conflict creates. That is understandable; in a crisis, to focus on anything else is a luxury. But in the midst of what seems like an endless stream of emergencies—a chronic state of crisis, as it were—it is clear that we need to transcend the crisis-management approach. Rather than becoming reactive, we need proactive strategies; rather than moving on when the rubble has cooled, we need a sustainable system to move survivors from conflict to peace, justice, and reconciliation.

It was this shared mission that first introduced me to the remarkable Heidi Kühn in 1997, in the early days of her dedicated efforts through Roots of Peace, her proactive, post-conflict strategy to restore dignity, opportunity, and hope to what has turned out to be millions in mine-affected countries around the world. While governments and military forces are vital to demining success, it has been a coalition of diverse groups—from nations to nongovernmental organizations, staffed with concerned, dedicated, and indomitable individuals like Heidi—which has succeeded in bringing the Ottawa Mine Ban Treaty into force in record time. It has been my privilege to join efforts at many levels and, indeed, to announce the critical fortieth ratification of the Ottawa Convention at the United Nations in October 1998, but I have been most inspired by steadfast activists like Heidi who are committed to addressing the suffering and devastation that prevent so many individuals and communities from recovering from conflict and building secure and peaceful futures.

Thank you, Heidi, for mobilizing your own impressively successful coalition of partners to transform the prospects of communities around the world and for contributing by promoting landmine awareness through your own personal story in *Breaking Ground*.

PREFACE

By Ken Rutherford

Professor of Political Science, James Madison University;

Cofounder, Landmine Survivors Network

On December 16, 1993, during a typical hot and dry day in the Somali desert, I was in my Toyota Land Cruiser, headed toward a refugee project site near the Ethiopian border. During the drive, as usual, I worked on my to-do list for the day—tasks like taking chicken cages to the airport so they would not be looted during my weekend leave in Kenya. Suddenly, the car shook and filled with dust. I could not see the papers on my lap; they had disappeared. As the dust cleared, I could see a foot on the floorboard. I wondered to myself, "Whose foot is that?"

I tried to step out of the cab, but my legs would not move. I grabbed the steering wheel, pulled myself out of the vehicle, and crashed down to the ground below. As I looked down at my legs, I saw that foot again. And I saw a lot of blood. I had become something rare for an American: I had become a landmine victim.

As I was lying on my back on the dry, hard ground of Somalia after my landmine accident, I stared up at the blue sky with white puffy clouds, the taste of blood in my mouth, and thought that would be the end of the line. Initially, I did not have time to be afraid nor fear death, but I knew it was coming. The lovely day had dramatically curved to an abomination, and my life would never be the same.

Little did I realize then, as I was trying to tie tourniquets around my blown-up legs and to radio for help, that *the world was in the midst of a global landmine crisis*. I did not know there were millions of landmines around the world waiting to be detonated.

Thanks to the incredible advocacy efforts of the many nongovernmental organizations comprising the International Campaign to Ban Landmines (ICBL), the Anti-Personnel Mine Ban Treaty was signed in December 1997, and, incredibly, more than twenty years after the signing of the treaty, we are celebrating the prohibition of landmines by a majority of the world's countries.[1]

Landmines contaminate sixty countries and areas. Hundreds of thousands of people continue living with the daily threat of losing life or limb.[2] Each year, thousands are killed and maimed—one-third of those children. Only 10 percent of those injured have access to health care and rehabilitation.

At the time of the treaty's signing, landmines were killing more than 24,000 people each year.[3] Even the US government highlighted

---

1. There are 164 state parties to the Anti-Personnel Mine Ban Treaty and one signatory—the Marshall Islands—that has yet to ratify. *Landmine Monitor 2018*. http://www.the-monitor.org/en-gb/reports/2018/landmine-monitor-2018/major-findings.aspx. Accessed October 9, 2019.

2. *Landmine Monitor 2018*. http://www.the-monitor.org/en-gb/reports/2018/landmine-monitor-2018/major-findings.aspx. Accessed October 9, 2019.

3. International Committee for the Red Cross, "Landmines Must Be Stopped," ICRC 1998, p. 16; *Deadly Legacy*, p. 308.

the global landmine crisis when the US Department of State estimated that between fifty-nine million and sixty-nine million landmines were deployed worldwide, thereby making them "one of the most toxic and widespread pollution[s] facing mankind."[4] For example, more than eleven years after the 1979 Soviet withdrawal from Afghanistan, where landmines were indiscriminately and randomly used, 150 to 300 civilians were injured by landmines each month, resulting in nearly 4 percent of the country's population disabled by mines and unexploded ordnance (UXO).

The signing of the landmine ban treaty took place in Ottawa, Canada, in December 1997. A half-continent away that same year, the humanitarian organization Roots of Peace was launched in San Rafael, California. Founded by Heidi Kühn, the organization dedicated itself to landmine action worldwide in an attempt to prevent landmine stories similar to mine.

Starting with a simple toast in the living room of her home and the desire to help the world plant the roots of peace, a global initiative was launched from the heart of a mother of four children after the death of Diana, Princess of Wales, who had catapulted the issue of landmines to the forefront of the international agenda.

Earlier that year, my fellow landmine survivor Jerry White and I had had the privilege of escorting Princess Diana to meet survivors in Bosnia. We had cofounded the Landmine Survivors Network the previous year as the first organization for landmine survivors by landmine survivors. Throughout her Bosnia visit, Princess Diana profoundly touched people affected by long-term conflict, poverty, devastating illness, horrific

---

4. *Hidden Killers 1998: The Global Landmine Crisis*, US Department of State Bureau of Political-Military Affairs, p. 9; *Hidden Killers: The Global Problem with Uncleared Landmines* (US State Department, Washington, DC, July 1993), p. 2.

injuries inflicted by landmines, and the ravages of war. She became the face of the landmine movement. The images of the Princess of Wales with landmine survivors were flashed around the world, drawing attention to the human wreckage caused by landmines and the need to both eradicate landmines and help the economic and social reintegration of landmine survivors. Princess Diana brought hope and inspiration to the living rooms of survivors in Bosnia and the global landmine crisis to the living rooms of the world.

Heidi's vision was to turn minefields into agriculturally productive fields. She believed that landmines were not only taking lives and limbs but also destroying one of Earth's most critical and fragile resources: its agricultural land. Her husband, Gary, was inspired to contribute his vast business acumen to help achieve this goal. Many areas infested with landmines had become economically unproductive and uninhabitable.

Heidi's innovative demine-replant-rebuild model offers a unique, holistic approach to restoring agricultural communities to vitality and self-sufficiency. Through its unique capabilities and partnerships, Roots of Peace has implemented programs in countries throughout the world that are rapidly and comprehensively restoring agricultural communities to stability and prosperity.

While I lost my legs to a landmine, I did not lose my life. The landmine accident in Somalia was actually a blessing for me in many ways. It allowed me to focus on what is important in life and not waste energy on trivialities. Far from making me reflective or wise, my accident made me appreciate what we can do with our limited skills and talents. When we focus on our beliefs and resources, we can accomplish amazing things. Heidi's Roots of Peace organization is an example of that. It is a story I have witnessed firsthand for two decades, and now, through her book, she is sharing it with the world.

Ever since that day in Somalia, I wake up every day as a landmine survivor. Yet, notwithstanding my own predispositions that may enter into judging what people are doing to alleviate the global landmine crisis, I attempt to be relentlessly impartial. In Heidi's case, there is no doubt that she continues to plant the roots of peace around the world, which, in turn, affirms all of us through her incredible dedication to perseverance and hope.

They shall beat their swords into plowshares.
And their spears into pruning hooks;
Nation shall not lift up sword against nation,
Neither shall they learn war any more.

—ISAIAH 2:4,
ETCHED INTO THE ISAIAH WALL OUTSIDE THE
UNITED NATIONS ROOTS OF PEACE GARDEN

PROLOGUE

On April 10, 2000, three young children were playing happily in Bosnia-Herzegovina. Ema, the girl, was eleven. Goran and Haris were a year older. Their families had lived in the area for generations. Then, following the breakup of Yugoslavia in 1991, when war broke out in the region that included Slovenia and Croatia, the families had fled, seeking shelter wherever they could for more than three years. With the official end of strife in early 1995, they were able to return home. Ema's, Goran's, and Haris's parents had warned their children to stay away from one particular hill when they played outdoors: During the war, soldiers had buried landmines throughout the area, and stepping anywhere could be deadly. However, the risk had not registered in the children's young minds; they wanted to frolic freely. They saw only colorful flowers waiting to be picked as gifts for their mothers, and they skipped down the hill.

Boom! Boom! Boom!

Their footsteps triggered one deadly explosion after another. Goran and Haris were killed instantly. Ema was fatally wounded. The sound of the blasts and Ema's cries had villagers and NATO workers running to the edge of the field. When Goran's and Haris's parents arrived, villagers restrained them from going to their dead children's bodies. Ema's mother and father arrived and were restrained by villagers, too, from running to their daughter. The horrified parents were forced to listen to Ema's screams for two torturous hours, unable to save her. A NATO team worked to clear a safe path to the wounded girl, but the field was thick with mines, and any move on their part risked detonating more of them. Ema died waiting for a path to be cleared.

This story made headlines around the world.

A tree was planted on a former minefield;
The trunk grew strong, and there was hope for a yield.
Branches became heavy with bouquets of fruit,
And thousands of farmers began to follow suit.
Millions of trees are now planted on former war-torn lands;
Children are educated, as their family livelihoods expand.
Farmers now sit content beneath the shade of the tree;
The Roots of Peace have been planted for all to see.

—HEIDI KÜHN

INTRODUCTION

---

*Coincidence is a miracle in which God
prefers to remain anonymous.*

—UNKNOWN

I'm not an everyday mom. I'll admit that up-front. All my life, I've taken risks, broken tough ground, and—as difficult as this is to admit—put my family at risk. How did I get this way? Part of it may be genetic: I come from a long line of pioneering women. Part of it may be good luck: I've had a lot of breaks. A big part of it comes from being stubborn: I don't know how to take no for an answer.

There is another reason why, all my life, I've been willing to take chances a more reasonable person would decline: I'm a believer. I believe in God, I believe in people, and I believe in myself. There have been life-threatening moments when even my stubbornness was not enough to save me, my children, my husband, or other loved ones from harm. Those were times when I knew from the core of my being that a Higher Power intervened.

I have no intention of making anyone reading this book into a believer. What I wish to convey is that we, as humans, are capable of doing great good in this world. It doesn't matter whether we see ourselves as ordinary or extraordinary, however those words might get defined. But I know, from a lifetime of real-world experience, that if your cause is just and your determination strong, you can achieve things beyond your wildest imagination. Let me tell you my story, and you can judge for yourself.

CHAPTER ONE

THE EPIPHANY TOAST

Ask, and it will be given to you.
Seek, and you will find.
Knock, and it will be opened to you.

—MATTHEW 7:7

One morning in January 1997, television news featured footage of Princess Diana walking through a minefield in Angola. The country had gained its independence from Portugal in 1975, but civil war had soon broken out and Angola had become an international battleground, with Soviet, Cuban, and American forces adding to the extreme tension. The end of the Cold War in 1985 did little to end Angola's internal conflict, with all sides escalating their purchase of weapons on the international market. By the time of Diana's visit, warring factions had buried millions of landmines across the country.

Diana was there to raise awareness for the work of the HALO Trust, an Anglo-American charity dedicated to removing explosives from civilian territories by engaging locals to rid their countries of mines. At the time, I remember wondering *Who is revitalizing the farmlands?* The television newscast showed Diana wearing protective clothing as she walked through the deadly minefields. That was inspiring: a British princess with the courage to step out of the trappings of her royal life to work with disadvantaged people she had never met in a part of the world she had never visited before.

Several years earlier, I had undergone treatment for cervical cancer and had made a deep promise before going under the surgical knife: "Dear God, grant me the gift of life, and I will do something extraordinary with my life." Princess Diana gave me a sense of what that something extraordinary might be.

I had been a reporter and producer for CNN in what was then the Soviet Union during my early thirties, and the diagnosis of cancer stopped me dead in my tracks. Cancer is a landmine for humans, just as explosive landmines are a cancer for the Earth. The remedy for both is removal.

Miraculously, I not only survived cancer surgery, but a decade later, I also became pregnant and delivered our fourth child, Christian, an affirmation of life after a potentially terminal disease. In August 1997, while nursing my healthy newborn son, I watched another television report about Princess Diana. This time, she was walking through the war zones of Bosnia-Herzegovina and visiting a hospital where doctors cared for children who had been maimed by landmines. Her next stop was the village of Tuzla, where she greeted a former soldier who had lost both his legs in a landmine explosion. In those days, the world called Diana "the People's Princess," a beautiful, fashionable woman with a heart for helping others. I admired this British royal whose interests extended way beyond England, a princess who had forged a place for herself as a global humanitarian.

On August 31, 1997, while fleeing paparazzi in Paris, Diana and her companion, Dodi Al-Fayed, died as the result of a tragic car accident. That day, the world lost more than a glamorous young princess; it lost its most vibrant advocate for eliminating landmines. Her death would impact innocent children whose lives might have been saved by her efforts. Diana stirred not only my political conscience but my maternal instincts as well.

It was around this same time that the Diplomatic Conference on an International Total Ban on Anti-Personnel Landmines, convened in Oslo, was finalizing a treaty intended to ban production, stockpiling, export, and use of landmines. Kofi Annan, then secretary-general of the United Nations, addressed the meeting only a few days after the world's brightest light for the landmine issue was extinguished. Soon after Diana's death, I learned that a small delegation was arriving in San Francisco for a reception intended to raise awareness of the treaty.

Unfortunately, just a few days before the announced reception, the delegation was informed that another event had already been booked at the proposed venue, the Commonwealth Club in San Francisco. It was an incredibly serendipitous moment, as there were many influential people in the region, but somehow, I was contacted. Aware of my international background as a former CEO of NewsLink International, working with various international news agencies, the organizers reached out to me by phone and asked if I would receive the delegation in my home. I enthusiastically agreed, but no sooner had I hung up the phone than it hit me: What had I just agreed to take on? Our house was a disaster, the result of four wild and carefree young children. How would I ever get the mess cleaned up, send out invitations, organize food and drink, all with a nonexistent budget? It had been an impetuous move on my part, but I'd been like that all my life—taking chances, attempting to do more than I should.

Responses were strong to my phone invitations. (This was in the days before the internet was widely used.) Even on short notice, more than a hundred people agreed to show up. As far as food was concerned, there was time after my children went to bed for me to make appetizers and hors d'oeuvres by hand. But wine was a bit more of a challenge. Our home was in Marin County, overlooking San Francisco Bay, near one of the world's great wine-producing regions. Guests from the region would expect me to serve the best if they were going to open their wallets to the anti-landmine committee. What to do?

Two days before the event, I was driving with my four children through the takeout lane of a local Burger King. My thoughts wandered back to my days as a reporter for CNN, which in turn churned up memories of a news story I'd produced about film director Francis Ford Coppola. The story had been seen by 17 million viewers, which put me in a good position to ask for a favor.

Two thoughts came to me as I sat in the car waiting for our takeout order. First, I should ask Francis to supply wine for the fundraiser, and second, it wasn't enough to just extricate mines from the land. We had to replace them with something. Why not grapevines? The thought of replacing death with life fit well with transubstantiation, the miracle of turning blood into wine that I'd learned about as a child going to weekly Mass. Images of a similar miracle danced in my mind: Blood was shed on vineyards in war-torn lands. Perhaps that land could be revived postwar, bear fruit, and be made useful once more. The laughter of my four children in the car brought me back to reality and only intensified the urgency of the vision to help make the land safe for families all over the world. My heart began to pound.

I called the team at Niebaum Coppola Winery in Napa Valley, and they reminded Francis of the CNN story. He remembered it fondly and graciously donated two cases of wine for the event. Encouraged, I called on two other friends, John and Desire Hart, who owned the winery Hart's Desire, and they donated a case. It had been Princess Diana's "heart's desire" to eradicate landmines, so the label was most fitting.

On September 21, 1997, three weeks after Diana's tragic death, the dinner party honoring the group of anti-landmine activists took place in my family home. One of the first to arrive was Jerry White, who had lost his leg to a landmine and had escorted Princess Diana to Bosnia-Herzegovina with Ken Rutherford only weeks before her fatal accident. After meeting purely by chance, these two American landmine survivors had decided to form the Landmine Survivors Network. Jerry was also a parent of four and had a great sense of humor. As he was introducing himself to my children, he casually took off his prosthesis. My children had met many guests to our home, including Japanese people who customarily took off their shoes, but no one had ever taken off a leg. This was Jerry's life, and he was not embarrassed about having lost a limb. He asked my children to escort him to a chair.

"Call me Robot Man," he joked so they would not be afraid. He told my oldest son, Brooks, "You always have to get up when life knocks you down." And with that, he grabbed Brooks by the arm and hopped to a chair by our fireplace, where he began speaking with other guests. The purpose of the reception was to raise awareness of the landmine issue, and Jerry had literally jumped right in. He told us the following story.

"In 1984," he said, "I was a young Irish Catholic boy from Brown University, twenty years old, hiking the Golan Heights with two American buddies. It was a beautiful day in April, and we'd wandered off the beaten track to camp on a beautiful hilltop. We didn't realize it was Tel Azaziat, a battlefield in the 1960s. The sun was shining, and the three of us were young and optimistic. Then, *boom!* I looked down and, to my horror, my leg was gone. 'My God, where is my leg?!' I exclaimed. The hilltop was a live minefield."

Pausing for emphasis, Jerry went on to explain, "My two friends managed to carry me out of there. Somehow, we made it down the hill without stepping on another landmine. It took me six months to recover in an Israeli hospital and learn to walk again."

He took another long pause to let his story settle in, then shifted gears back to his later tour of Bosnia-Herzegovina with Princess Diana. "I invited her to come as a commoner, which meant not as royalty. She beamed and said, 'That sounds like heaven.'

"Of course," Jerry went on, "the British security wasn't happy about what they thought of as Diana's impulsive decision to travel with Ken Rutherford and me to Bosnia. We were glad they relented. It turned out to be her last visit to a minefield."

He grew sad as he described her funeral in London and personally watching Diana's boys, Will and Harry, bravely walking behind her casket. He told us how proud the boys were when he described for them their late mother's compassion for others. Jerry's stories moved everyone present. I felt a shiver run down my back when I realized my own boys were the same age as Will and Harry.

The evening continued with a presentation by the anti-landmine advocates. They were exhausted from their travels, but their voices were strong and their words powerful. When they finished, Dr. Michael Pelfini, a kindergarten friend and neighbor of mine who had become a respected pianist, performed "Candle in the Wind," the song Elton John had sung only a few days earlier at Princess Diana's funeral in Westminster Abbey. There was a deep reverence in the room, and each note reminded me of the sadness experienced on the day John F. Kennedy was assassinated. On that historic day, my classmates and I at the Dominican Garden School were sent home after being told by our teacher, Sister Patricia, to pray for peace. I lifted my glass and softly offered a toast.

"May the world go from mines to vines!"

It was meant as a simple summary of the challenge before us, but it came out like a well-prepared metaphor. Where did it come from? I had had a high fever earlier in the day, and maybe that had raised images in my mind. Native Americans often call it a fever dream, but to me it was a very clear vision. My husband and four children looked at each other in surprise. The room was silent. Slowly, guests gathered around, encouraging me: "Mines to vines! You must take that message to the world!" they said. I nodded politely. It took a while before I could consider that this just might be the fulfillment of the promise I'd made when going into surgery for cancer: to do something extraordinary with my life for the sake of others, and to make my footsteps count. By removing landmines, we could ensure that millions of innocent footsteps would be free of risk. And by replanting the seeds of life, we could heal the wounds of war. Landmines are a cancer on the one Earth we all share, and we must remove them for sustainable life to flourish once again. It was an epiphany.

The emotion of the evening was palpable. At the end, as Jerry White stood at our family front door, he impulsively reached into his jacket pocket and gave me his own photograph of Diana, taken in a minefield in Bosnia-Herzegovina only a few weeks before. "You have the heart of the Princess," he said, "and it is your responsibility as a mother to take this vision out of the living room of your home." It was a defining moment, and I faced a choice: I could rest on the laurels of a beautiful evening, or I could take the aura from my backyard into the world. With no blueprints for peace, I chose the latter.

Mines have been killing innocent people for hundreds of years. At the time of the reception in our home, there were somewhere between 70 million and 110 million landmines buried in seventy or more countries. Another estimated 250 million landmines were stockpiled worldwide. On average, every twenty-two minutes of every day, someone stepped on a landmine. These devices killed or maimed more than 26,000 people each year, nearly half of them children. At the then-current rate of extraction, it would have taken 1,100 years and $33 billion to clear them all. The more I learned about the crisis, the more I felt compelled to do something.

On October 10, 1997, only a few days after the mines-to-vines toast, the Norwegian Nobel Committee awarded the Peace Prize to the International Campaign to Ban Landmines (ICBL) and campaign coordinator Jody Williams. Ambassador Hans Ola Urstad of Norway had been in the living room of our family home, and when I had shared my dream, he had told me that attaining it was highly improbable. Yet overnight, the subject of landmine removal had been published and broadcast worldwide.

A few weeks later, I was invited to the New York Marriott Marquis Hotel to attend the UNA-USA Global Leadership Award dinner. This annual event, sponsored by the United Nations Association, a nonprofit organization that supports the United Nations, that year honored Ted Turner, CEO of CNN. (A gala dinner for *Wine Spectator* hosted by Marvin Shanken, the magazine's publisher, was also held there that weekend; the concept of "mines to vines" appeared to be taking root.) Stunning a black-tie audience of diplomats and dignitaries at the award dinner, Turner stood up and offered $1 billion to the United Nations, saying, "Let's not turn our backs on the world; let's join hands and change it! Indeed, we have no other choice." Turner designated the funds to benefit programs aiding refugees and children by clearing landmines and fighting disease, and the United Nations Foundation was formed.

In addition, I was introduced around the room and, as inspirational conversations flowed, a vision for the concept of transforming minefields into vineyards worldwide began to come into focus.

In November 1997, I again imposed on our vintner neighbors, this time to join me as witnesses to the historic signing of the Convention on the Prohibition of the Use, Stockpiling, Production, and Transfer of Anti-Personnel Mines and on Their Destruction, also known as the Anti-Personnel Mine Ban Treaty, scheduled to take place in Ottawa the following month. More than 160 countries had agreed to sign, but 32 had refused, including China, Egypt, Iran, Iraq, Pakistan, Russia, Turkey, and the United States. By attending the signing with me in Ottawa, the Napa Valley vintners would be demonstrating their concern for farmers around the world who risked their lives to harvest grapes in landmine-infested fields. Humbly, I approached the world's most prominent vintners and shared my dream.

The convergence of the untimely death of Princess Diana, news of the awarding of the Nobel Peace Prize to the ICBL and Jody Williams, and Ted Turner's $1 billion gift had catapulted the issue of landmines to the forefront of the international agenda within weeks, and three compassionate California winegrowers agreed to walk with a mother armed only with an idea to transform mines to vines. These included legendary vintner Robert Mondavi, who sent his Canadian national manager; Tor Kenward, senior vice pesident of Beringer Vineyards; and Eric Wente, owner and CEO of Wente Vineyards.

When I sought the advice of Mondavi, a visionary icon, he looked clear into my eyes and told me, "My path was simple: Follow your passion. Pour in your heart and soul. Settle for nothing less than excellence. And with enough hard work and faith in yourself, you can realize your dream." Breaking ground on new ideas was nothing new to Mondavi; he helped turn Napa Valley into a world-famous wine-growing region, and saw the valley grow from just 17 wineries in 1976 to over 400 wineries two decades later. Standing in front of the statue of St. Francis at the entrance of his winery, he encouraged me to follow my dream to transform minefields into vineyards. Gazing over the autumn harvest, Mondavi proudly stated, "I feel blessed. So many men and women search and search but never find their passion, their calling, their sense of mission that would ignite their hearts and fill their lives with meaning and joy." He told me to go turn my mines to vines.

That evening, I announced to my husband, Gary, that I'd be traveling to Canada to witness history: the signing of the Anti-Personnel Mine Ban Treaty. He looked at me blankly. There was no need for him to state the obvious: With four small children, we had no money to spare for such adventures. He was right, so I took a full-time job as US marketing director for a Canadian ad agency named Plan B with a plan of my own: to save my paychecks to finance my vision. The next month, I packed my bags for Ottawa. The landmine issue had captured my heart, as I felt no mother should ever have to hold a child in her arms who had lost a limb to hidden seeds of terror. This deeply resonated in my soul.

It took only one day of exposure to freezing Canadian winds to realize that, as a nursing mother of a two-year-old child, I was not prepared for the toll this trip would take. I quickly developed a high fever and mastitis. It was painfully uncomfortable, but nothing compared to what landmine victims endure on a daily basis; left in place, landmines would continue to claim civilian victims even after the combatants had withdrawn.

The gathering drew representatives from 122 countries to sign the treaty. While international news chastised the United States for not signing the Ottawa treaty, the Canadian papers noted that my small group of California vintners was in attendance to show our support for fellow farmers around the world who deserved to cultivate a harvest of hope—without fear.

It was at that event in Canada that I first met Jody Williams, and where she boldly stated, "I believe that people can do extraordinary things when they think about the greater good." Those words deeply resonated with me, as the ICBL and Williams had started a process that, in the space of a few years, transformed a ban on antipersonnel mines from a vision to a feasible reality. Other global luminaries and dignitaries, such as Kofi Annan and Lloyd Axworthy, Canada's minister of foreign affairs, filled the room, and their deeply inspirational words fanned the flame for my fledgling vision to turn mines to vines.

"Landmines are among the most barbaric weapons of war, because they continue to kill and maim innocent people long after the war has ended," Annan said. "Also, the fear of them keeps people off the land, and thus prevents them from growing food." I knew at this moment that I had to dig deeper for peace.

As soon as the signing event was over, I flew home, feverish but glad to be back and taking care of my children.

December was a merry-go-round of parental duties: driving our two-year-old son to see Santa Claus, chauffeuring our daughter to daily rehearsal for the Marin Ballet's production of *The Nutcracker*, picking up the two older boys in muddy uniforms from their winter soccer tournaments—days were long. I woke at 5 A.M., spent two hours handling paperwork in our basement office, flipped pancakes around 7 A.M., packed the children off to school, and then packed myself off to work at Plan B, visiting clients in Silicon Valley, a two-hour drive from Marin County. The salary from my job helped cover the growing costs of our basement mines-to-vines office, including long-distance telephone bills and expensive international mailings.

My biggest concern was that I was spending less and less time with our children. In wanting to help children around the world, was I sacrificing my own? Was I spreading my energies too thin? The questions were, in a sense, irrelevant. On weekends, when our family went for walks along the beach or down mountain trails, it was impossible to avoid imagining what it was like for parents walking with their children through minefields, unable to trust the very earth beneath their feet. All children deserve to walk without fear.

I had no clear path or business plan, only the conviction in my heart and a growing sense that I had been called to accept a mission that was much larger than me. My thoughts veered from faith to fear.

On New Year's Day in 1998, I went on a morning hike with our family friends Joseph and Mary Cresalia and their nine children. As we hiked down from the top of Mount Tamalpais, my youngest nestled snugly in my backpack, I expressed my concerns: "Joe, I'm so conflicted about having become preoccupied with removing landmines. It feels like this mountain but bigger and steeper. If I fail, it's a long way to fall."

Joe was a successful businessman and a dedicated father, and I was pretty sure he would tell me to get off the mountain and go back to my family. Instead, he looked me in the eyes and said, "You have no choice. This is your life's journey." He went on to tell me that my plans for ridding the world of landmines were not a preoccupation, but an important mission. He predicted that people would be there along the path to help and that I should not be afraid.

"What you need first," he said, "is an attorney to register you as a nonprofit and draw up bylaws and articles of incorporation." All of that was foreign to me. Start a nonprofit company? I'd never done anything like that, and I had no money to hire a lawyer. At that very moment, a man came walking up the path from Stinson Beach. He greeted us and we struck up a conversation. It turned out that this Iranian-born gentleman, Keyvan Tabari, was an international attorney, and, on hearing our dilemma, he offered then and there to help set up the nonprofit company at no cost. Like so much else surrounding Roots of Peace, he was utterly heaven-sent.

The original name for the organization was Mines to Vines, inspired by the spontaneous toast at that first fundraising dinner, but since then, I had received a shocking piece of news. Earlier that year, I'd introduced a UN executive to my Napa Valley vintner friends. In discussions with them, he heard the name Mines to Vines, stole it, and filed it as part and parcel of his organization. I immediately called him to insist that this wasn't fair.

He laughed and said, "You were the one who introduced me to those California vintners. Now they're my contacts. Who do you think they would rather work with, a housewife or the UN? They don't need you anymore. Turning minefields into vineyards is big business. You stumbled onto a good idea, Heidi, but it's time for you to go back to being a housewife, back to your children."

I was crushed.

Yet when this person reached out to the California vintners to whom I had introduced him, the wine owners demonstrated their integrity by remaining loyal to me. When the person in question found out, he became hostile. I had made my first enemy. There would be others in years to come, many of them much more dangerous.

Not to be dissuaded, I turned to colleagues at Plan B, the Canadian advertising company where I worked, and the creative staff there came up with a new name for my project: Roots of Peace. The concept was bigger than "mines to vines" and more deeply evocative of the entire planet. This time, having learned the hard way, I followed the advice of my many experienced advisers and quickly registered the name.

As my wise Granny McNear always used to say, "Success has many fathers. Failure is an orphan."

Meanwhile, there was so much pushback against the United States for failing to sign the Ottawa treaty to ban landmines that the State Department created a new entity to deal with landmine issues: the Office of Weapons Removal and Abatement in its Bureau of Political-Military Affairs (PM/WRA). In February 1998, the director of the affiliated Office of Mine Action Initiatives and Partnerships, Jim Lawrence, called and I picked up the telephone just as my children were coming home from school. Laughter and screaming were in the background, and I could barely hear the voice on the other end of the line. When I called him back from the refuge of my basement, I realized that Lawrence represented a government agency making a serious offer to partner with me and the California vintners. What a thrilling development! I agreed immediately, and we began a series of weekly calls.

These calls were always early in the morning, the only time my otherwise chaotic home was quiet. My aunt Nancy Menary, who lived next door, told me that she often gazed out her window when she woke up at 5 A.M. and could see my basement lights burning brightly. I explained that New York City and Washington, DC, were three hours ahead; there was no choice but to start before sunrise. She was a wise woman and a pioneering feminist, and from then on, she often bounced up the family trail to prepare breakfast for our children or drive them to school so that I could work.

During those first years of Roots of Peace, I managed the day-to-day operations from our basement, using a shoebox for financial receipts, surrounded by friends and neighbors. They would ring the doorbell, and I'd open the door in my lavender slippers with rhinestone hearts, which we jokingly called my "Queen of the World" magic shoes, and escort everyone downstairs to our "Worldwide Headquarters." (We needed any edge we could get, and humor helped.) I would run back upstairs and pack lunches for my children and walk them to school, then hurry back downstairs to join the others. We worked from 9 A.M. until 3 P.M., when I fetched the kids from school and drove them to their various after-school programs.

The big event of 1998 was the launch of the newly incorporated Roots of Peace. We had critical help for the launch from Mitch Werner, who had been recently appointed to the office of UN secretary-general Kofi Annan. Mitch was the former director of the United Nations Association of the United States, a nonprofit group that oversaw various UN projects (and had sponsored the event honoring Ted Turner that I had attended the year before). He had taken a keen interest in Roots of Peace after watching my tenacity in dealing with the political obstacles placed in my path. One day, he called with an idea.

"The secretary-general is planning to come to the West Coast on UN business," he said. "Why not invite his wife, Nane, to launch your new charity? The worst that can happen is that she says no." Exciting idea.

I consulted with Dr. Noel Brown, former director of the North America regional office of the United Nations Environmental Programme (UNEP), and with the newly appointed UN NGO liaison, Peggy Kerry, sister of US senator John Kerry. Both encouraged me to pursue Mitch's idea.

In between my children's naps and their playground visits, I drafted a letter of invitation to Nane Annan. After finalizing the letter and signing it, I faxed it from my basement office to the secretary-general's office on the thirty-eighth floor of UN headquarters in New York City. During my calls to his office, I had befriended Maria Reyes, a secretary in the office at the time, and she assured me that she would personally deliver the letter of invitation to Nane Annan.

Soon after, I received a call from Gillian Sorensen, the UN assistant secretary-general for external relations, whose husband, Ted, had been senior adviser and counselor to President John F. Kennedy. Ted was instrumental in the creation of my favorite childhood quote, "Ask not what your country can do for you. Ask what you can do for your country." Gillian requested detailed information about the event—the number of guests, location, security, and other related matters—then we said polite goodbyes. I had no idea what would happen.

Late one night the following week, I heard a familiar beep coming from the basement, which meant that the fax machine was preparing to receive a document. What now? Would there never again be a moment's peace in the Kühn home? Resigned to another sleepless night, I stumbled down the stairs and watched as the printed fax page emerged—and there at the top of the page was the UN logo. It seemed to take forever coming out of the fax machine, but sure enough, it was a letter of acceptance from the office of His Excellency Kofi Annan. Nane Annan had agreed to attend the launch of Roots of Peace.

The United Nations had its beginnings in the San Francisco Bay Area, where the original delegates had gathered beneath the towering redwood trees of Muir Woods on May 19, 1945. After World War II, President Franklin D. Roosevelt had dubbed these sacred trees "temples of peace" but had died before his vision could come true. My grandfather, Bill Thomas, was president of the Rotary Club of San Francisco, the second-oldest chapter in the world, in the early 1940s and had witnessed the signing of the Charter of the United Nations at the War Memorial Building in San Francisco. It was fitting that Roots of Peace was also based in the Bay Area, a location with a long legacy of innovation for peace.

But once again, as had happened with the trip to Ottawa, the excitement of the moment was doused by a cold bucket of financial reality. We were now faced with the task of funding a reception that included the wife of the secretary-general of the United Nations. My ambitions were always a mile in front of my pocketbook and perceived business skill.

To receive donations for the event, Roots of Peace had to be a non-profit organization, a legal position we had not yet achieved. Help came from the Marin Community Foundation's new CEO, Dr. Thomas Peters, who took the initiative of registering Roots of Peace as an official fund of the foundation, a status that enabled us to legally host the launch event. Ursula Hanks, director of the American Red Cross in Marin County, also stepped forth to offer her credible NGO status to enable Roots of Peace to host the fundraiser.

Providence also stepped in to help, just as Joseph Cresalia had predicted it would on that morning hike a few months before. Bobby Muller, president of the Vietnam Veterans of America Foundation, learned of our predicament. He understood the suffering caused by landmines and pledged $10,000 to cover the cost of our event. Our friends George and Paula Tuttle also helped sponsor the event, and Jennifer Puff from the Marin Education Fund and Alix Derby from the Marin Community Foundation guided me through the beginnings in starting an international charity. Henry Dakin, founder and CEO of the Foundation for Social Innovation, offered sage advice and strong encouragement. And Kathy Geschke Orciuoli reached out to technology leaders in the Silicon Valley community. With funding secured, we reserved the World Trade Club of San Francisco's private dining hall, located on the waterfront of the scenic San Francisco Bay. It was the perfect place to launch our mission with leaders of the United Nations.

Back at home, I shared my vision with another mother, Helga Krogeness, while we waited for the dismissal bell to ring to pick up our older children in the parking lot of Glenwood Elementary School. We both had three-year-old toddlers, and we watched them play on the grass while we talked world peace.

Helga told me about her Norwegian mother, Brit, who had had her own vision for peace. When war broke out in the Balkans in 1992, Brit had boldly stated to her daughter, "We are building a Viking ship—a ship of peace. We will turn war into peace!"

Helga looked deeply into my eyes and told me that I reminded her of her mother, and she encouraged me to carry my vision forth. The next day, she called with great enthusiasm to inform me that, serendipitously, her mother's boat was coming to San Francisco in a few weeks. "Why not include this wooden Viking boat at the entrance of the waterfront to welcome Mrs. Nane Annan and honor her Scandinavian roots?" exclaimed Helga.

After attaining approval from San Francisco Mayor Willie Brown, we just had to wait for the ship to arrive from Oslo and dock in Oakland, and for its passengers to be transported to the entrance to the Ferry Building. In the meantime, we had a lot of work to do.

This was all in April 1998, before the explosion of emails and social media, and printed invitations were needed to properly get the word out. Our basement crew flew into action, designing and mailing the invitations along with stamped return envelopes. Within a short time, we had received more than 200 confirmed RSVPs. While the event would be expensive, Bobby Muller's pledge alleviated that particular anxiety.

At that same time, another supporter of our efforts, Matt Lorin at the State Department's PM/WRA agency, put us in touch with his contacts at Warner Bros. The studio was involved in the making of a comic book that warned of the perils of landmines, so it seemed like a natural partnership. Matt's introduction led to an invitation to host another event. This one would be on the Warner Bros. lot where television series such as

Little House on the Prairie and *Bonanza* had been filmed. I called people at the Napa Valley Vintners Association (NVVA), and they agreed to supply fine wines for the evening and bring the legendary names behind the labels to pour for guests.

My next call was to various businesspeople I knew to get their advice. Which event should we do, I asked, the World Trade Club's event or the one on the Hollywood set? Instead of recommending one over the other, they told me that I should do both. That would show my ability to bring together two important California groups, they said: the harvesters and Hollywood.

"Who's going to refuse an invitation to sample the best Napa Valley wines on a Hollywood set?" they argued. "All you need to do is show up." Then the NVVA offered to take responsibility for securing a good turn-out through its own channels, with radio announcements and outreach to high-level mailing lists from dozens of established wineries.

It sounded like a good deal, but my deeper intuition told me to be cautious. I'd grown up in the San Francisco area and had personal access to lifelong friends in that region. In Los Angeles, however, I had no such contacts. But with only three weeks to go, I allowed myself to be lured into signing an agreement that made me financially responsible for a costly event. If successful, the Hollywood gathering would be a grand prelude to the event in San Francisco with Nane Annan, but would it be possible to get a good turnout with just three weeks' notice? I was being encouraged by people with experience in such matters. Or so I thought.

On the evening of April 16, I flew to Los Angeles to host the event at Warner Bros. I walked onto the studio lot and was met by an eerie silence. The only noise was the clinking of wine bottles and glasses as the Napa Valley vintners set up. Minutes grew into hours. No one showed. It was one of the worst feelings I'd ever experienced. To this day, I will never know if someone set me up to fail—perhaps the people who advised me to do both events wanted to put an upstart woman in her place—or if I was just the victim of my own naive optimism. Either way, the onus was on me for having believed something I had sensed to be wrong. I'd signed on the dotted line as head of the beneficiary NGO and was now responsible for repaying $60,000 in costs.

Getting on the airplane back to San Francisco the next day was painful; sheepishly, I walked down the aisle as the vintners who had supplied wines for the event glared at me from their seats. I kept my head down, avoiding eye contact. My heart was filled with shame. I felt like an impostor.

The debt was bad enough, but worse was that I had only a few days to rally for the next event at the World Trade Club in San Francisco. All expenses had been paid up-front, so at least, this time, that pressure was not on me. Sherri Ferris, owner of the event-organizing agency Protocol Professionals, knew of my circumstances and took charge of preparations for the event. For example, she invited business representatives from various San Francisco consulates to greet Nane Annan as a way of honoring her Scandinavian roots. Sherri also arranged for red rose petals to be placed at each table setting to be symbolic of the teardrops of mothers who had lost children because of landmines.

Unlike at the Hollywood disaster, 200 guests attended the launch of Roots of Peace in San Francisco on April 20. I'd chosen an ice-blue suit and was horrified when Nane Annan arrived wearing a suit of the same color. An American Red Cross representative noted my discomfort and reassured me that matching dress was a positive sign. Apparently the late Princess Diana had worn a gown the same color as that of Elizabeth Dole, wife of Senator Bob Dole of Kansas, when they had appeared together at a similar press event to speak about landmine issues. It was, he assured me, a good omen that Nane Annan and I were on the same page.

Our head table consisted of luminaries from the world of anti-mine activism, including Jerry White and Bobby Muller, and legendary vintners, including Nancy Cope of Robert Mondavi Winery. Our local San Francisco congresswoman, Nancy Pelosi, was seated to my right. "I will be with you in your vision for turning mines to vines," she whispered to me, "for however long it takes to do it." Little did I know that her offer would extend far into the future, when she would be twice elected the country's Speaker of the House. She invited me to attend both of her swearing-in ceremonies (2007 and 2019) with her grandchildren.

The Marin Girls Chorus, which included my ten-year-old daughter, Kyleigh, had taken the day off from school to attend the event and sing the inspirational Prayer of St. Francis, "Make Me a Channel of Your Peace."

Make me a channel of your peace
Where there's despair in life, let me bring hope
Where there is darkness, only light
And where there's sadness, ever joy

The World Trade Club event was a stunning success, and afterward, I didn't owe anyone a penny. But how would I pay for the failed Hollywood party from four days before?

That summer, my husband, Gary, took our family to Europe with miles earned from his various business trips. He knew how hard I'd been working and how disappointed I'd been by setbacks beyond my control. The trip coincided with the return of our oldest son, Brooks, from his freshman year at Marin Catholic High School. The chance for us all to be together on a memorable journey across Europe served as a good reminder: Without the psychological comfort of knowing that we have attended to the needs of our nearest and dearest, we can't feel comfortable attending to the needs of our global family. You've got to put on your own oxygen mask before you can help others with theirs.

Father Kevin Longworth, our family priest, had recently retired from St. Sylvester's Church in San Rafael and moved to St. Patrick's Church in Kiltegan, County Wicklow, Ireland. Knowing that our trip was intended to heal and restore us for the mission ahead, he invited us to visit Ireland. Gary needed to return to work, but my kids and I gratefully accepted the invitation.

St. Patrick's Church is nestled on the side of a lush mountain. From there, we set out with Father Longworth on a tour of the local villages. Whenever we came across farmers driving their animals across narrow roads, he yelled out, "Cow crossing!"—sending the children into fits of laughter. One day, we drove by intuition and arrived on a hilltop where we met dozens of refugees from Kosovo who had been nestled in isolation and had never interacted with the local Irish community. We spent a memorable day with them, even though no English was spoken, and invited them to a nearby fair at St. Patrick's in County Wicklow. To the astonishment of the community, we sent buses from Dublin for them to enjoy the music, dancing, and local dishes, which inspired the simple yet profound reminder of how different and also how similar we humans are.

One morning, we drove across the southern shores of Ireland to a remote church that featured an altar with carvings of bogs, the country's signature wetlands. In earlier times, trees were considered sacred and linked with saints. Bogwoods were often retrieved from boglands, where they had been buried for thousands of years.

"The roots of Ireland don't go any deeper than its bogs," Father Longworth told me. "Your mission is like that—very deep, very important. Don't let setbacks slow you down. I've watched you over the past three weeks with your children. Your vision is sincere and comes from the depth of your heart. Help will come from above. Just carry on. Carry the cross."

As though prompted by the father's generous words, the next day a proclamation of support for our work arrived from Pope John Paul II, addressed to the "Foundress of Roots of Peace." It seemed that others had been watching our footsteps from afar at the Vatican. Quite a parting gift!

Upon my return, the good people at the NVVA made a generous offer to work with me on a better-organized event from which all proceeds would go to paying off the Hollywood disaster. The new event, which took place in October 1998 at the Fairmont San Jose, was a big success. We paid off a good portion of the debt—and I wrote off a good portion of my disappointment about it. It was time to break new ground!

Roots of Peace had become a nonprofit, tax-exempt organization in April 1998, and with official papers in hand, we resumed our fundraising efforts. In May 1999, Robert Mondavi and his wife, Margrit, hosted a fundraiser for our project in the private dining room of the Robert Mondavi Winery in the heart of Napa Valley. It gave Robert Mondavi great satisfaction to host the event, because he had once believed he could make great wines equal to the greatest wines in the world, even though everyone said it was impossible. He saw that same spirit in me as

I took on the daunting task to eradicate landmines and plant grapevines worldwide.

More than one hundred guests attended, including Jerry White; Donald Steinberg, the former US ambassador to Angola at the time; Lieutenant General Robert Gard, president of the Monterey Institute of International Studies; and actor Armand Assante. Cast members from *Phantom of the Opera* performed and filled the room with a sense of greatness as Robert Mondavi described his fine wines paired with a five-course meal. Seated next to me, he shared personal stories about the perseverance and passion needed to turn ideas into reality. Don't be afraid to fail, he told us, be afraid not to try.

Finally, he rose, lifted his glass, and with a strong voice echoed my initial toast, "May the world go from mines to vines!" That night, we raised $30,000, enough to finance the demining of our first field. At last, for the time being, we were back in the financial "plus" column.

Step by step, Roots of Peace was making progress. I applied to George Soros's Open Society Foundation and received a $15,000 grant that allowed us to expand our fledgling office and afford airfare to attend conferences at UN headquarters in New York City. It was around this time that the United Nations Association launched its Adopt-a-Minefield initiative. Sir Paul McCartney and his wife, Heather Mills McCartney, who happened to be an amputee, led the campaign and engaged the support of many Hollywood celebrities. To my delight, Roots of Peace was the first organization to contribute to the Adopt-a-Minefield project, funded by a generous donation from our friend Robert Mondavi, and matched by the Bureau of Political-Military Affairs's Office of Weapons Removal and Abatement. In consultation with State Department officials, we determined that our first program would be in the Medari Vineyards of Dragalić, Croatia. On the southern border of Nova Gradiška near Bosnia-Herzegovina in a winemaking region that had been heavily mined during the Balkan War, the vineyards were a perfect initial mines-to-vines location.

In the first month of the new millennium, the time had come for me to take footsteps in an actual minefield with a clear intention of creating a more peaceful world for future generations to thrive in. It was time to walk the talk.

On January 6, 2000, my husband, Gary, asked me to meet him at his new office in Berkeley, where he'd been hired by a new tech company named StarQuest after having worked for IBM, Adobe Systems, and Autodesk for more than a decade. That day was my birthday, and when I arrived, Gary generously handed me his Visa card and told me to buy a warm jacket for the upcoming trip to Croatia as my gift while he finished a meeting. Near his office was a North Face Outlet Store. When I got there, I noticed a sign over the entrance: "Never Stop Exploring." I walked in and, in a stern voice, asked to speak to a manager. A nervous sales clerk paged the manager to come down and speak with me.

When the manager arrived, I firmly explained that I had a problem with the motto posted on the front of his store.

"I'm departing for Croatia in a few days as part of a US State Department mission," I told him. "Did you know that after the Balkan War, there were more than a million landmines planted throughout Croatia? Did you know that once-beautiful countryside has been a field of death ever since, and that most of the victims are innocent farmers and children?

"If I were to follow the advice of the North Face and 'never stop exploring' in Croatia," I continued, "I would likely get blown up. How can anyone explore fields that are riddled with landmines?"

The North Face manager began to perspire ever so slightly as I explained that Croatian farmers lived in freezing cold weather and were unable to cultivate their own farmlands because of landmines. "Where I'm going," I said in conclusion, "they can't afford to clothe their families, much less 'never stop exploring.'"

The manager excused himself and quickly stepped away, and I wondered whether perhaps I'd come on a little too strong with my intuitive words. I'd been excited, nervous, and a little overwhelmed about the trip, and I feared it had gotten the best of me.

Ten minutes later, he came back with an armful of new winter jackets.

"I'm deeply touched by your story, madam," he said, explaining that he'd called his boss at North Face headquarters and that the company had decided to donate $50,000 worth of coats and other supplies for the Roots of Peace mission to Croatia. "Can you please drive to the back of the store? We'll help you load your car."

An hour later, I drove out of the North Face store's parking lot and arrived back at Gary's office. He happened to see me pulling up in our SUV, which was overflowing with as much of the new gear as it could hold, and he let out a scream—very unlike him.

"What have you done?" he yelled out his window. "You were supposed to buy one coat, not the entire store. Have you lost your mind?"

I parked, walked into his office, and explained what had happened. Gary looked at me with tears in his eyes and immediately organized a convoy of vans to pick up the rest of the newly donated winter items from Berkeley's North Face Outlet. In all, the donation filled twenty vans with merchandise. Later that day, there were coats and tents and a store's worth of other goods scattered all over our living room floor, and that evening, Gary made me a really great birthday dinner, toasting my vision.

However, we soon realized there was another problem. My flight was departing in six days, and it was painfully obvious that it would cost a fortune to ship these items from the United States to Croatia. I called an old friend from San Rafael High School, Kevin Loughlin, who I remembered worked at Federal Express; it turned out that just the week before, he'd been promoted to head of global distribution.

Perfect!

Then he added that, coincidentally, Federal Express had recently established an office in Zagreb, Croatia.

Double perfect! What were the odds?

He added, however, that it would be extremely expensive to ship so much merchandise so far, and the possibility of FedEx getting everything there in time for our arrival was more than we could hope for. Then, once again, the heavens intervened to help us, as they would so often over the coming years. I can't really explain how or why this happens, but I do believe in the power of prayer. Kevin took the next few days off to negotiate with his FedEx management team, and I took every advantage to see the conversation through. Sure enough, FedEx coordinated delivery of our goods in record time to Zagreb. The company had never flown the route before, but after hearing what it was for, the good people at FedEx headquarters in Memphis agreed to take on the challenge—at no cost.

The job wasn't over yet. We had to itemize each ski jacket, each fleece overcoat, each sleeping bag, and each pair of shoes for the customs forms. Word went out, and friends arrived at our hilltop home in droves: the Bainbridges, the Campbells, the Dolls, the Hoyes, the Hunters, the

Kagins, the Loughlins, the McNears, the Menarys, the Murphys, the O'Malleys, the Pelfinis, the Rubinis, the Saribalis, the Sebastians, the Tabusis, and the Tuttles—all equipped with pens and tape dispensers. Their children used colored markers to decorate the boxes with hearts and flowers. When at last we'd finished 300 boxes, we set them in the driveway for shipment.

A Federal Express truck came barreling up our road, and we watched with awe as burly workers loaded the boxes and drove away. Would everything really arrive on time in a place FedEx had never serviced before? It was now out of my hands.

The next day, I packed my things for the long trip to Croatia. Saying goodbye to my children was definitely the hardest part of leaving, but as I drove away from them and toward the airport, I remembered that my dear Granny McNear, who had died at age ninety-six just a few years before, had left me her beautiful home on one condition: I had to do something for peace. She had a favorite saying: "Trust in the Lord with all thy heart, and lead not unto thy own understanding. In all thy ways trust in Him, and He will direct thy path." That path was taking me away from my children in the first month of the new millennium and into deadly minefields. I needed to trust in Him more than ever.

There would be a number of distinguished men and women with us on the Roots of Peace inaugural mission in Croatia. My husband enlisted Bill Rus and Rich Koch, two top business leaders at Autodesk, a former place of employment, who now worked with MapGuide software, which could help modernize landmine detection. Carol Bartz, the CEO of Autodesk, fully supported our efforts in the Balkans. "I'm often asked if technology really matters," she told a reporter for a story about our mission. "Our partnership with Roots of Peace shows that it does. We can leverage technology to assure that a child can safely walk across a field in Croatia." Carol assigned her public relations department to hire a videographer to join us and document our work.

I invited Ann Laurence, whom I had met at the Rotary Club of San Rafael and who had been a member of Another Mother for Peace during the Vietnam era and understood the agonies of war firsthand. Victoria Stack, a Washington, DC, philanthropist, also agreed to join us. On the flight as well would be Jim Lawrence of PM/WRA; Donald "Pat" Patierno, director of the Office of Humanitarian Demining Programs (also part of the State Department's Bureau of Political-Military Affairs); Ali Gallagher, a psychologist; and Bill Wood, a global-mapping specialist. The Roots of Peace delegation departed in January 2000 with solid footsteps for peace.

I didn't know it then, but before my return, someone would place a bumper sticker on my car that read, "This is no ordinary housewife you are dealing with!"

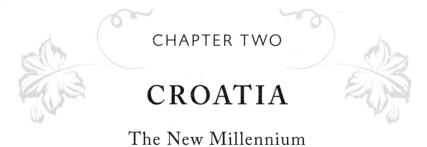

CHAPTER TWO

CROATIA

The New Millennium

Greater indeed than the creation of man
is the creation of the heavens and the earth.

—THE HOLY QUR'AN (40:57)

In January 2000, when our plane touched down in Zagreb, the damage at the airport revealed just how devastating the Balkan War had been. The airport was barely functioning, and recent tragedies were written on the people's faces. Two drivers greeted us: George, a husky ex-soldier, and Rocky, a stocky former boxer. They would be not only our drivers but also our protectors.

Our destination was the Sheraton Zagreb Hotel, where Slobodan Milošević had stayed only a few weeks prior to our visit. Milošević, president of Serbia from 1989 to 2000, had recently been charged with war crimes by the International Criminal Tribunal for the former Yugoslavia. Adding to the tensions of the moment, the former president of Croatia, Franjo Tuđjman, had died less than a month before; we were arriving at a transitional moment for the country. The streets of Zagreb were lined with posters of candidates for the upcoming presidential election, including images of Stjepan Mesić, who favored Croatia's transition to a market economy, and there was concern about social unrest.

Our tight schedule began with a formal military briefing at the office of Bill Montgomery, the US ambassador to Croatia. His British wife, Lynn, was an admirer of the late Princess Diana and took an active role in leading our Roots of Peace delegation.

To our amazement, by the time we returned to our hotel, a FedEx truck had arrived to deliver the 300 boxes of jackets and winter gear from the North Face. My husband had given me a credit card with which to buy one jacket, which had multiplied into hundreds. In the first month of the new millennium, it seemed like a miracle on the order of the biblical story of the loaves and fishes.

We piled into well-worn minivans, and George and Rocky drove our delegation forty miles from Zagreb to the city of Sisak, where we met the director of the Croatian Mine Action Center (CROMAC) and its experts gave us a briefing on the current status of mine clearance in their country. Using colored pens, deminers marked trees and rocks in mine-infested fields to indicate where they had left off the day before. Areas that still contained mines were marked in red. Other colors were used to indicate to children where it was "safe" to walk.

Our colleagues from Autodesk were astonished to learn about the center's archaic and dangerous methods of landmine removal. More sophisticated processes began with the formal gathering of mine-related information, including minefield records if available, data about mine victims, and interviews with former combatants and local people. Technicians then created detailed maps to guide clearance operations. Only then, after the required information had been assessed, was the appropriate technology and personnel for the job determined. Properly trained and equipped deminers then stepped onto the live field and used metal detectors and long, thin prodders to locate the mines. It is a silent process as deminers go inch by inch, combing the land. Concentration is critical: One misstep could be their last. The deminer kneels, pushes the prodder into the ground, and listens for a loud beeping sound that signals the presence of a landmine. From a distance, it looks as if he is praying. When a mine is located, the technician steps away and the mine is detonated. The process is then repeated until every landmine has been removed from the field.

The Roots of Peace advisers from Autodesk donated expensive MapGuide software that increased the speed and efficiency of mine removal. Within ten years, in large measure thanks to the advanced Autodesk software, Croatia would progress from a war-torn nation to one of the most popular tourist destinations in the world.

After the briefing, we took our first steps onto a live minefield. The day was freezing cold. We exited our van and were greeted by Croatian deminers shivering in the morning wind. I asked one of them why he did this job, and he answered that he had two young children.

"If I do not do the demining, who will protect them?" he asked.

From our supply, I presented him with a North Face jacket. The deminer broke down and cried, explaining that during all the years of fierce conflict, he'd never had a decent jacket to keep him warm. The jacket, he said, would be a badge of honor.

Nothing could have prepared me for the stark reality of walking through a live minefield. My heart began to race as the field officer explained that decades-old mines are as dangerous as when they were first laid, capable of exploding at the slightest pressure. Most of the mines are hidden, but if you know what you are looking for, you'll have a better chance of avoiding them.

"Don't let your guard down!" exclaimed the CROMAC officer. There was absolute silence as the wind whistled through the deadly field. "Constantly be on the lookout for trip wires, as these aren't usually clearly visible, so you've got to look closely at the ground. Wires are usually thin enough to be almost impossible to see." We continued our intrepid, careful footsteps as we walked directly behind the professional deminers deminers, our faces ashen. We saw dead animals in the distance, and we were told that it takes only eight pounds of pressure to detonate a landmine, and many of nature's beasts had also been victims of these deadly seeds lurking in the soil.

Damaged vehicles and abandoned cars were also visible, and we were informed that those were sites where landmines had possibly exploded and must be avoided until the land was demined. With each footstep we took, we felt the gravity as we imagined the life that had once thrived on these war-torn fields.

"The moment you realize you may be in danger, freeze! Do not take another step. Take some time to assess your situation and formulate an escape plan. Your movements need to be slow, careful, and considered." That is what they explained to us and the surrounding villagers.

As I reached down to pick up a child's stuffed toy left along the trail, the deminer shouted, "Stop! Many mines are booby-trapped. You may think you are picking up a helmet or toy, and there often may be a land-mine deliberately hidden inside—it is bait meant to lure and blow up a child." I froze, horrified.

The bone-chilling words were aligned with the cold winter weather. Step by step, in our protective gear, I continued to walk with my friend Ann, from San Rafael's Rotary Club, and we shook our heads in disbelief. Together, we remembered Rotary International's Four-Way Test, a moral code: "Is it the truth? Is it fair to all concerned? Will it build goodwill and better friendships? Is it beneficial to all concerned?" Walking through our first minefield, we realized it exemplified a contempt for each of those principles. Together, we wondered how we could possibly convey our horror to our Rotarian friends back home in Marin County and garner their support to take action for the removal of landmines worldwide. But this was our quest.

From Sisak, we drove to Dragalić, where the Medari Vineyards were located. During the four-hour drive, we observed towns and fields marked by years of war, homes leveled, roofs destroyed, telephone poles downed, front yards bleak and lifeless. Located on the border between Bosnia-Herzegovina and Croatia, Dragalić had seen major battles and everyone there had lost someone: a child, a parent, a sibling, or another relative.

We arrived to find the mayor standing in the cold, waiting for us. Enthusiastically saluting the foreigners who had raised the money to remove landmines in the fields surrounding his remote village, he escorted us into a chilly conference room, where we were greeted by a group of village farmers. We sat around a large table and took turns introducing ourselves. There were flags in the center of the table representing both Croatia and the United States, and there was hot tea that we all greatly appreciated.

An older woman dressed in black approached me and clutched my hand. "Thank you," she said through an interpreter, "for choosing our town." She gazed at me sorrowfully and added, "The war ended, but the landmines are still here."

I held her strong hand as the translator continued relaying her words. "My husband and I were at last able to return to our farm," she said. "It was winter, and we were planting carrots and potatoes to survive. He turned on his tractor, and within a few moments there was a sudden *boom!*"

Her sad blue eyes bore into mine as tears welled.

"No woman should have to pick up her husband in a thousand pieces because his tractor rolled over a landmine," she said. "I thank you because my grandchildren will never have to suffer such a fate."

It was a stark awakening. Ann and I looked at each other and thought the same thought: While we had been committed to the mission of Roots of Peace before coming to Croatia, our conviction had been theoretical. Hearing directly from people affected by landmines in their own backyards made the effort very real.

We said our farewells to the group of farmers and were escorted next door to a grammar school where many of the students had been orphaned by the war. Fifty or so of them lined up in the hallway and greeted us with a song. Our translator, Dushka, explained that the song described the perils of landmines and the hope that someone would come to heal the wounds of war.

"It would seem their prayers have been answered," Dushka said.

A young blond boy about ten years old, wearing well-worn jeans and a tattered sweater, approached me and asked, "You are from California?"

"Yes," I told him, "Why do you ask?"

"I only saw California in movies," he said through our translator. "There are no landmines there?" I shook my head.

"Then it must be like heaven," he said.

Our hosts drove us up a dusty road to meet a local Croatian family to see what life was truly like living in a minefield. We were greeted at the front door by Matko, the father, who invited me into his home, where I met his wife, who was preparing a traditional dinner as a gesture of gratitude for our efforts in eradicating landmines in their country.

As we walked outside, I was aghast to see their five children tethered to poles as they played and laughed. In another context, it looked like a dark version of a maypole with hungry children wearing tattered clothing dancing around dirty ropes—a truly chilling version of childhood. Shocked at the scene, I asked their parents why they tethered their children to poles instead of letting them play in the panoramic fields of their backyard.

They looked at me blankly. "Respectfully, Mrs. Kühn, the entire backyard you see is riddled with landmines. If we do not tether our children, they will be tempted to retrieve the only family ball when their parents are not looking." My face became ashen as they continued, "We are being good parents, as we do not want them to lose their limbs to a landmine while playing."

It was impossible to avoid thinking about young people who enjoy summer vacations back home in Marin County—hiking Mount Tamalpais, sunning themselves on Stinson Beach—and how meeting the boy who asked me about California, or these young children tethered to a macabre maypole, might move them to do something for children elsewhere in the world, young people like themselves but with none of their privileges.

Often I would overhear my children's friends say, "We're bored!" during their summer vacations in California. Yet a world away in Croatia, these children in front of me could only dream of playing a sport without losing a limb or risking death to a hidden landmine. As I listened to these innocent words, I desperately wanted to return home and teach my children not to live their lives in a bubble and to remind them, once again, "For unto whomsoever much is given, of him shall be much required."

A few years later, in the fall of 2004, I returned to visit Matko and his growing family. My daughter, Kyleigh, accompanied me to see the progress made since her first visit, in 2000.

When we arrived, we watched with awe as Matko's children ran freely without restriction through their backyard, which was filled with colorful flowers. Their mother had baked fresh bread with wheat grown on former minefields, and the aroma of peace filled the room. The jam was made with berries grown in their fruit orchards.

Together, we sat down with their neighbors. The fruits of our labor were clear as Matko made a toast—"*Živjeli!*" (the Croatian word for "cheers")—to our efforts of transforming mines to vines in the heartland of Croatia, and our glasses clinked as we all shared warm smiles and reaffirmed our vision of planting the roots of peace throughout the world.

After our first visit to Matko's family, we drove to the site of the Medari Vineyards, where our demining operation was scheduled to begin. On the way, we saw a rusted basketball hoop on a dirt playground where children were forbidden to play. Surrounding the area were bombed-out homes, and beyond the homes was an empty sports field, also abandoned because of mines. People stared at us from behind shattered glass windows. I often wondered what these local children must have felt as they peered out their family window at forbidden basketball hoops and sports fields—the promise of play always out of reach, the knowledge that retrieving a rogue ball could end their lives in a split second. Night began to fall as we drove past the ruins of a church. Looking closer, we saw that its large cast-iron bell had been pierced by a mortar shell, but the steeple had somehow managed to remain intact. A full moon shone over the church, and amid the rubble, the steeple glistened in the moonlight—a symbol of hope.

We drove another three hours from Dragalić to Vukovar, a village on the banks of the Danube River. Our guide informed us that the war had turned neighbor against neighbor, and in Vukovar alone, 154,000 homes had been destroyed. When a truce was finally declared, only four homes remained standing. We drove through the city's decimated streets, and it was impossible to guess what most of the buildings had once been. In Vukovar, the Serbs and Croats had lived together for generations, and there had been frequent marriages between members of the two closely related ethnic groups. To ignite hostilities between them, however, Serbian dictator Milošević had given speeches reminding them of ancient hostilities, describing battles that had been fought as far back as the 1300s. Inflamed by his speeches, the Serbian-dominated military attacked unarmed citizens of Vukovar. As our van drove on, we saw a giant water tank in the center of town, riddled with bullet holes, preserved as a testament to the horrors the town had endured.

George and Rocky drove us to a nearby hospital, where a doctor described the time US secretary of state Cyrus Vance had visited the hospital to meet with representatives from the local government, who assured Vance that no atrocities were being committed there. Meanwhile, in the basement, militia members were loading 180 patients into vans and transporting them to a nearby pig farm to be slaughtered and buried in a mass grave. When Vance toured the hospital, he found the rooms empty.

We drove from the hospital along the same road, to the same pig farm, to the same mass grave of 180 innocent Croatians. Ann and I held hands. For two Americans who knew war only from watching television in our comfortable homes, this confrontation with mass murder shook us to the core. We sank to our knees on the icy ground and said prayers for the victims and their families.

"The good people buried in this mass grave did not die in vain," we prayed. "May God give us his blessings to help realize peace on Earth so that their families will not suffer as they did."

Rising up, we saw the image of a dove etched into a monument commemorating the dead. That was where the idea came from to have a dove of peace with intertwining grapevines as the Roots of Peace logo. It was created by Heward Jue, then a designer at Digitas.

From Vukovar, we drove to the home of a ten-year-old boy who had lost his right leg to a landmine. He and his parents greeted us at the door of their modest home, and the boy lifted his pants leg to show us where his leg had been severed at the knee. He was in great pain from a recent surgery to prepare him for a prosthesis, but still he managed a smile, and through our translator, he thanked us for visiting his home and helping other children escape his fate. He had a sweet voice, and the moment was overwhelming for Bill Rus, who saw in the boy a reflection of his own two sons, who were about the same age. With tears in his eyes, he presented jackets to the boy and his family members.

As before, expressions of appreciation for our gifts were overwhelming. The new jackets, waterproof and insulated, were made of state-of-the-art Gore-Tex, which could withstand freezing cold and driving blizzards. The boy and his parents had never owned anything like them, and their faces lit up. The boy explained to us that the jackets meant more than winter protection. There was no work for miles, and his father did not earn a living, yet now, with such attractive new coats, he and his family could appear in public with dignity. He was wise beyond his years.

We left Vukovar and returned to Zagreb, driving through the night. We arrived late but were too energized to sleep, so I stayed up talking with a new friend, General Tulecik. The Croatian War of Independence had been fought from 1991 to 1995 between Croats and Serbs, and Tulecik had fought on the front line of the conflict, which he referred to as the Homeland War. More than 20,000 people had been killed on both sides, and more than a half-million people had been displaced. People who had been neighbors for generations threw one another down deep wells and committed other severe acts of aggression. We were uneducated about these realities and hungry to learn and understand. He told us how Croatia had been a pristine land, yet even now, years after the peace agreement, there were still more than a million active landmines planted throughout the country.

The next morning, we drove to the sister villages of Cista Mala and Cista Velika. Mala's population was heavily Serbian, and Velika's largely Croatian. With the war looming, citizens from both areas had made a pact to remain friends. Then Serbian forces arrived in tanks. Soldiers had decorated their gun barrels with bright flowers as a ruse to trick villagers into thinking they'd come in friendship. Unprovoked, the tanks opened fire, killing hundreds of innocent bystanders. After that, the Serbian forces laid landmines up and down the borders. During our visit, villagers on both sides begged Roots of Peace to demine their lands for the sake of their children. After the customary meet-and-greet, we distributed more jackets to shivering villagers just as snow began to fall.

Vjekoslav Majetić, owner of vehicle manufacturer DOK-ING, met us and demonstrated a newly designed tractor that could be remotely operated to remove landmines in large, open areas. In wide, flat fields, the machine was practical. However, in mountainous areas, where there were vineyards and trees, deminers would have to remove landmines in the traditional, labor-intensive manner: step by step, and by hand.

We continued on to Zadar, a city along the Dalmatian coast. There, too, villages had been devastated by landmines, and remnants of blown-up homes littered the landscape as far as the eye could see. We noted something curious, however. In the rubble of each neighborhood, there were piles of destroyed cooking stoves. When I asked why the stoves remained, our hosts explained that when enemy forces approached, families would prepare to leave, turn on the gas, close all doors, and let the house explode. The Croatian townspeople found leveling their homes preferable to leaving them to be occupied by Serbian forces. It was their way of fighting back in a war that pitted neighbor against neighbor.

In Zadar, we gathered for an annual celebration of Croatian culture. Traditional songs, dances, and food and enlivened the room, symbols of life. It was a refreshing change after many days of exposure to the realities of war.

Our official visit to Croatia was over, and I sat with Pat Patierno, who works for the US government to deliver programs and services aimed at reducing the harmful effects of illicitly proliferated, and indiscriminately used conventional weapons of war. He was convinced that Roots of Peace still had important work to do in Croatia, as so much of the country remained in need of landmine clearance. We sat down with our Autodesk colleagues and, calculating all the in-kind contributions from the company, as well as FedEx and others, we came up with a total of $360,000. Then Pat wrote on a white napkin that the State Department would make a matching grant if we returned to continue the work.

Our efforts during those first days of 2000 were beginning to show signs of success. Of course, everyone on the mission missed their families, but that first trip had shown us that the dream of turning mines to vines could become a reality in the new millennium.

As Rotarians, during our visit Ann and I asked to visit the Rotary Club of Zadar, in a beautiful community located along the panoramic coastline of Croatia. Both of us were mothers and wives who had clear intentions of leaving a legacy of peace for the next generation.

When we arrived at the Rotary Club of Zadar, we could see visible signs of war in the men's faces. Many had clearly fought hard, and it showed in their haunted eyes.

Rotary is a humanitarian nonprofit, and we, as Rotarians, were deeply committed to eradicating landmines and restoring hope to the lives of these people who had already suffered so much. We wanted to bring the bountiful vineyards indigenous to the Dalmatian coastline back to life.

Branislav Brkic, president of the Rotary Club of Zadar, had his own part in revitalizing the coastline of the Adriatic Sea. Architect Nikola Bašić wanted to design a sea organ, an instrument made of tubes located underneath a set of large marble steps—an architectural wonder and instrument that would be played by nature itself. Brkic created the foundation for this sea organ and helped Bašić turn his idea into reality. As we continued to transform mines to vines in his homeland, he worked to help lay the groundwork for a musical instrument played by the wind and the waves of the sea. It was a duet of sorts as we challenged each other to achieve our dreams.

Throughout the years, Roots of Peace worked tirelessly to raise funds with the Rotary Club of San Rafael in a four-way match with the Rotary Club of Zadar. Together, we have restored the vineyards and partnered with the University of Zadar to grow fine wine on former battlefields.

Each year after that first visit to Croatia, I returned to Zadar with dreams of restoring vines to war-torn lands and music to the seas. It seemed, at times, like an impossible dream. Then, in April 2005, the sea organ became a reality, and today, thousands of tourists walk freely on former minefields, and they may touch their toes in the Adriatic as they listen to the sounds of a dream accomplished.

As we drove back to Zagreb for the last time before returning to the United States, we had a few moments to walk through the beautiful city and experience some of its history and culture. The city's tenure as the capital of the Habsburg Kingdom of Croatia had had a profound impact on the architecture, and when Ann and I walked past the train station to the top of a nearby hill, we discovered majestic St. Stephen's Church. Inside, we gazed up at a large statue of the Blessed Mother Mary and, again, bent to our knees in prayer.

My dedication to Mary started when I was quite young. When John F. Kennedy was assassinated in November 1963, my classmates and I were sent home from kindergarten by our teacher, Sister Patricia, at Dominican Garden School in San Rafael, and she'd asked us to pray for peace. That night, I had a profound dream of the Blessed Mother with her translucent face shining on me. Her golden light radiated a message of "Peace, peace, and only peace" and has never left my heart. That dream has stayed with me ever since and is embedded in the name Roots of Peace, which, like so much of life for believing Catholics, is an act of transformation.

Throughout my life, I've seen many paintings and statues of Our Lady, but never one that reminded me of that special dream as clearly as the statue in St. Stephen's. This moment was an affirmation that I was on the right path with my vision of transforming mines to vines worldwide.

I continue to see statues of Our Lady with her serene face, and she is often standing on a globe of the world surrounded by white roses and stepping on a serpent. From my heart, it is her grace that is needed to step through the many minefields of the world.

CHAPTER THREE

SECOND MISSION TO CROATIA

Footsteps for Peace

For the Lord will restore the splendor of his creation,
even though devastators have devastated it
and destroyed its branches and vines.

—Nahum 2:2

In February 2000, shortly after I arrived home, I was invited to meet Miljenko "Mike" Grgich at a Grgich Hills Estate dinner served by famous Napa Valley chef Bob Hurley. Mike was born on the Dalmatian coast in what is now Croatia, so it seemed fitting to discuss our mines-to-vines program with him. Upon my arrival, I was honored to be seated next to him at the head table by his executive assistant, Maryanne Wedner, who encouraged me to share my vision with this legendary vintner. For hours, Mike told me the story of his early years in California, when he was a humble vintner working with Robert Mondavi and Chateau Montelena. I was fascinated with our conversation, as I vividly remembered when the Eurocentric wine world had suffered, screamed, and raged with shock that wines made on California soil were comparable to French wines.

Mike, in his thick Croatian accent, recited the history of origin of the infamous Paris Wine Tasting in 1976. "Steven Spurrier, a wine expert from England who ran a fine wine shop in Paris, decided it would be fun to organize a blind tasting to coincide with America's Bicentennial celebrations in 1976. For the tasting, he gathered together the best French judges and the finest French wines, and to salute America on its 200th anniversary, he added a few wines from some upstart winemakers in California. André Tchelistcheff and Jim Barrett hand-carried the armload of California wines to Paris for the competition at the Inter-Continental Hotel.

"The judges expected to sniff and gag when they tasted the California wines, but it did not happen that way. The nine French judges blind-tasted the white wines and graded each of them. The winner was the Chateau Montelena Chardonnay that I had made. The French judges were speechless, and a few tried to suppress the results, but without success," Mike exclaimed with pride.

Mike told me he had received the news that he won via a congratulatory telegram, and he still hadn't been quite sure exactly what had happened, but he knew that something significant had taken place. "Then my phone rang and *Time* magazine called me. As an immigrant, I told him that I had done nothing wrong! 'My taxes were paid, I've done nothing illegal, and your journalists have no business calling me.'" The phone went silent. Then the journalist continued, "Congratulations, Mr. Grgich, you have won the Paris Tasting!"

As the famous Grgich Hills Chardonnay was served with dinner, Mike continued to share his intimate story with me, and I listened with great intent. "It was more than good luck, as it was truly a miracle in my heart. Luck is the product of preparation and opportunity." This moment was far more, as the Paris Tasting revolutionized the wine world and shattered the myth that only French soil can produce world-class wines. California's victory also inspired other winemakers in different parts of the world by exposing the fallacy of French superiority and giving new hope and energy to winemakers in Australia, Chile, Italy, New Zealand, South Africa, and even Mike's beloved Croatia. Then, on July 4, 1977, Mike partnered with Austin Hills, owner of Hills Bros. Coffee, to break ground and establish Grgich Hills Estate in the Napa Valley.

As dessert was being served with a fine glass of Violetta—named for Mikes's daughter, Violet—he peered into my eyes and asked me, "Why are you taking on such a dangerous job to eradicate landmines, when you could just remain in the Napa Valley and enjoy the abundance of life?" Tears welled in his eyes as I told him the firsthand stories of his homeland, which was now riddled with over 1.2 million landmines, and as I described the importance of respecting the soil and the soul, which must be demined and freed from those dormant seeds of hatred.

"Soil and soul. Both must be cleared, Mr. Grgich, so that good seeds may restore the Earth and transform the human spirit with seeds of hope in war-torn lands." I took a deep breath as I realized I was sitting next to the most famous vintner in the world, who knew of miracles from the soil. Then I added, "From the depth of my heart, this is how we plant the Roots of Peace."

It was a risky moment to pour my passion out like that, yet I trusted my instincts.

Mike was a deeply spiritual man, and he appreciated the significance of replacing landmines with vineyards, symbolically turning blood to wine. To my astonishment, our conversation turned into a deeply spiritual discussion as he shared that his sister often visited Medjugorje in the former Yugoslavia to pray at the Queen of Peace statue, where the Virgin Mary is said to have appeared to the children in 1981. The concept of planting the Roots of Peace took on a deeper meaning, as Mike shared that he too had had a vision of the Blessed Mother, in his homeland following World War II, when he escaped the Communist regime. In the vision, a cross had appeared on the horizon, guiding him on a journey to California. It was not a story he shared with most people, and it was his way of telling me that Roots of Peace was a mission we would pursue together.

I showed him photos of our time in his homeland and he wept, realizing how the vineyards of his childhood had become zones of death. The year before, Mike had purchased property in Trstenik, located south of the city of Split and north of Dubrovnik, with the goal of teaching fellow Croatians how to support their families by growing fine wine. I invited him to be a part of our mission in his homeland.

"I will help you on one condition," he said. "I want to travel with you back to Croatia."

Around this same time, I shared the Roots of Peace vision with another renowned Sonoma Valley vintner, Judy Jordan, owner of J Vineyards and Winery in Healdsburg. I showed Judy, the mother of two small children and a successful businesswoman, photos of our first mission to Croatia, and she offered to do whatever she could to help, as she was also a deeply spiritual woman, and the concept of turning mines to vines deeply resonated with her. By the end of our first meeting, she was also ready to join Roots of Peace on our next trip.

I contacted Jim Lawrence from the State Department's PM/WRA and advised him that I would be returning to Croatia in the spring with two prominent vintners, and he offered to once again join our delegation. We discussed a date for this second stage of our mission, but his availability in early May conflicted with my daughter Kyleigh's thirteenth birthday. My children had already sacrificed a lot over the past two years, and I was not about to miss her becoming a teenager.

Later that afternoon, I was the designated soccer mom, driving the girls home after practice, and I listened to my daughter talk with her friends about the latest pair of designer jeans and what dresses they should wear for their upcoming eighth-grade graduation. It was at that moment that I decided to invite Kyleigh with us as the youngest delegate on our mission to Croatia. Here was an opportunity for her to see firsthand the true challenges in life as she prepared to enter Marin Catholic High School. Such lessons could not be found in textbooks. It would be a valuable rite of passage for a young woman entering her teens. I prayed that it was not also a well-intended mother's foolish plan, one that would expose her daughter to some of the most dangerous conditions on Earth. She was my only daughter, and I wanted to raise her with character and give her the tools to navigate the world, but there were no blueprints for how to do that. I had to trust that this was the right decision.

In my effort to be a good mother, I hosted a Hawaiian-themed thirteenth birthday party for Kyleigh and her friends to bring a sense of normalcy into our home, carving watermelons and sewing handmade flower leis for my May Day baby. As the Hawaiian music played, the front doorbell rang. Frankie Frost, a photographer with the *Marin Independent*

Journal, stood at the entrance, arriving to take a picture of the pile of single boots I was collecting in my basement for landmine survivors in Croatia.

I had this pile because, on my previous visit, I had realized that there were many landmine victims who literally did not have a leg to stand on, but they still needed shoes for their remaining foot. So I set out on a quest to gather single shoes from various stores around town, which would normally discard their stock when there was not a matching shoe. It was a terrible waste to throw them away, especially when landmine victims could use these shoes. A new, high-quality shoe could provide them with a sense of dignity that might enable them to walk tall, even with only one foot. Over the months, I had gathered quite a large pile from sympathetic Marin County store owners.

When I answered the door to greet Frankie, dozens of teenagers were dancing with hula hoops on the lawn. At that moment, I realized that I too was dancing between many worlds, from Marin to the minefields.

In May 2000, the flight to Croatia was desperately long, and Kyleigh, exhausted, slept most of the way.

Sixteen hours later, we touched down in Zagreb, and we were quickly spirited away and given a formal briefing at the US embassy. Ambassador Bill Montgomery and his wife, Lynn, invited Kyleigh to spend the night at their home. Their daughter was the same age as Kyleigh, and they intuited that the girls' time together would be a wonderful team-building experience. What an opportunity for Kyleigh! Here was a chance to enhance her interior landscape, as my Granny McNear used to call it—a unique chance to set her moral compass for life.

Kyleigh accepted the invitation to join us in large part because of a newspaper story she'd read about those three young children killed in

Bosnia-Herzegovina who I mentioned in the preface of this book—three children among thousands of Bosnian children killed by landmines. To detonate a landmine takes eight pounds of pressure. That was about what my Kyleigh weighed when she was born.

There is a silver lining to that desperately sad tale. When Kyleigh's friends, who were Girl Scouts in Marin County, read the story in the *San Francisco Chronicle*, their leader, Lisa Hoye, asked them which philanthropic cause they would like to support with the proceeds from that year's Girl Scout cookie sales. Unanimously, they agreed on Roots of Peace, and the funds went toward demining the field in Bosnia-Herzegovina where those three young children had died. When the International Trust Fund for Demining and Mine Victims' Assistance learned about this gesture by the Girl Scouts, the international organization matched the Girl Scouts' contribution. Today, there is a Roots of Peace Garden growing on the demined field where the three Bosnian children lost their lives.

This was our second trip to Croatia, and we began by returning to Sisak after the night in Zagreb. During a briefing in Sisak, the director of the Croatian Mine Action Center showed us the progress CROMAC had made in the five months since our first visit there. Antiquated methods of identifying minefields with colored markers had been replaced with Autodesk's MapGuide software, and engineers were quickly and accurately tracking the locations of mines. Once a field had been cleared, farmers were able to safely cultivate their land. Gradually, the pristine coastline of Croatia was being restored and tourism was beginning to flourish once again. Finally, we could see with our own eyes that our efforts were having a visible impact.

Unlike during our previous visit in January, the May temperatures were soaring into ninety-degree heat. Seventy-eight-year-old Mike Grgich took off his outer shirt in the back of the van and enjoyed the ride to Dragalić in his white sleeveless T-shirt. Mike was a hero to the people of Croatia—the local boy who had done well. There were no helicopter flights available, so on this trip, he was one of the "ordinary" people traveling in a large van with no air conditioning.

The mayor was there to greet us on our arrival, along with a crowd that burst into applause. We'd brought art supplies for the local schoolchildren, including giant white canvases, and we invited the children to paint their childhood dreams on the canvases and include a pictorial history of their memories. The results were dramatic. If this exercise had been done back home in California, children might have painted flowers and butterflies. In this beleaguered part of the world, the children painted achingly vivid images of war: broken telephone lines, dark fields with landmines hidden in the grass, and bursts of red representing the bloody consequences of stepping on one. We carefully wrapped the canvases and brought them back to California, where they served as effective tools for raising funds at the Sonoma Academy, a college-preparatory school located in Santa Rosa, which many of the children of supportive vintners attended. Later, we dubbed the effort "paintbrush diplomacy."

My daughter, Kyleigh, paid homage to her home by bringing a piñata in the shape of a sun on the trip. The principal of the school was thrilled at this multicultural gesture and gathered the children in the sports field Roots of Peace had recently cleared. The children were blindfolded and took turns swinging a bat at the piñata filled with candy. The first child was a brave young girl who seemed hesitant to be blindfolded after suffering the traumas of war. Finally, she took a swing, and the students cheered with laughter as she hit her target. Each child was given a turn swinging at the piñata, and Kyleigh saw for herself the effects of reaching out beyond the constrained borders of our California home.

Next, we visited the Medari Vineyards, where grapevines grew on war-torn minefields. Mike Grgich was visibly moved watching the land-mine removal funded by his dear friend Robert Mondavi. On the other hand, nothing had yet been done to prepare the land for replanting the destroyed vineyards. This was the spring planting season, so we moved quickly to increase agricultural training and replanting, and soon local farmers were again planting fields that had been inaccessible during many years of war.

At our next destination, Vukovar, Mike identified another major site for landmine removal: the fields of Ilok. Located along the scenic Dan-ube River, Ilok was the burial site of St. John of Capistrano. Together, we attended Mass, and local vintners celebrated the arrival of their native hero. The Croatian language is foreign to me, but Christian traditions are the same everywhere, and Mike smiled with pride at the statue of the Blessed Virgin Mary that presided over the site. Together, we placed a white rose at her feet and prayed for her blessing in our effort to trans-form mines to vines.

A few miles away were the terrorist camps of Arkan, a Serbian war-lord known for giving orders for ethnic cleansing, who had died in the first month of 2000. The fields where he had fought were the same sites where some of the world's best white wine was grown—Grasevina, Syl-vaner, and Traminac—along the panoramic Danube River. According to local lore, the queen of England had once traveled to this region on a white horse specifically for the taste of these wines. Now, the vineyards were riddled with landmines, and we were determined to remove them.

We returned to Zagreb and said farewell to Mike as he continued his annual vacation in his hometown of Trstenik, along the Dalmatian coast. The remaining members of our group continued on to the western region of Zadar, where we visited the Roots of Peace–funded demining team in the fields of Cista Mala and Cista Velika. Five months into the project, these lands once held hostage by landmines were being successfully cleared. The mayor hosted a banquet in the center of the town to celebrate our arrival, and toasts of "*Živjeli!*"—"Cheers!"—were made around the table as Croatian and Californian vintners touched glasses.

Following the luncheon, the villagers escorted Kyleigh and me to the home of a young woman who had lost both her parents in the war. The woman, newly married, had given birth to a little girl. As we entered her home, we heard the baby crying. After asking the mother's permission, Kyleigh picked up the baby girl and held her close to comfort her.

The moment brought back a memory of Kyleigh as a newborn herself, crying like that, struggling for life in an incubator at Marin General Hospital as a consequence of having contracted a potentially lethal Group B strep infection during delivery, an outcome of my cesarean section. I remembered how I had asked my four-year-old son, Brooks, to choose from a box of toys a gift I could give his failing sister. It was a painful moment, but the nurses told me that it was best for a sibling to have closure. "Please, Brooks, darling, just pick a gift for your baby," I had softly told him. I remember how he had moved as though his hand was being guided. Then, his soft brown eyes looked up at me, and he chose the tiny pink wooden crucifix I had carried as a child to my first Holy Communion. Back in the hospital, our family priest, Father Longworth, began administering last rites to our little girl. Brooks placed the tiny crucifix in his sister's incubator and said, "This is what my baby needs."

The nurses told me that it was time to leave, but I instead sat in a rocking chair and began to pray with all my heart. It was the Feast Day of Our Lady of Fatima, when three Portuguese children had received apparitions of the Blessed Virgin Mary in 1917 in a small village north of Lisbon. I clutched my rosary beads while holding the hand of Father Longworth as warm tears flowed down my face and I prayed for a miracle. Within moments, Kyleigh's vital signs began to improve. The doctors were at a loss to explain why she had taken this turn toward life.

Thirteen years later, Kyleigh stood holding a Croatian baby girl as small as she had been back then. No longer the awkward little girl, Kyleigh was now a gangly teenager wearing a red kerchief and cutoff jeans. For the moment, life felt like it had come full circle.

The demining team called to us from outside the window. Kyleigh gave the baby a kiss on the head, and we all drove to the edge of the area, where a dirt road backed up to a vineyard. I got down from the van and followed Vjekoslav Majetić, a diminutive man with gray hair, a little gray mustache, and a sparkle in his eyes whom I had met during my previous visit. He was the director of DOK-ING, whose technological advances in robotics had taken demining to new heights of safety and sophistication. Kyleigh stayed behind to watch her mother make the trek through cleared minefields.

With Majetić as my guide, I began to climb through the rocks toward the recently cleared vineyards to see the fruits of our efforts. The aroma of fresh lavender filled the air, and sprays of purple blossoms dotted the countryside. Several men stood at the entrance of the demined field, wearing helmets and white protective clothing that resembled a cross between an astronaut's suit and a beekeeper's gear. I wore ballet-style slip-ons and khaki capris and felt lighthearted and proud that our efforts had made a difference in this beautiful place.

Majetić motioned me to follow him up a steep incline. Grasping cool, craggy rocks, I pulled myself up the narrow pathway that led to the vineyard, stepping up the pace as I became more confident of my footing. In the distance, DOK-ING's robotic tractor ground its way across an adjoining field, engaged in methodical cleanup work. Majetić's large handheld radio crackled with Croatian dialog as he monitored his team's work.

We reached the top of the rocky section of the path and emerged onto a wide-open field. Just as my muscles began to release from the exertion of the upward climb, behind me the voices on the radio got louder and faster, taking on a sudden urgency. Majetić said something that sounded like a question, and a volley of replies shot back. He went pale.

"Mrs. Kühn, stop walking," he told me, making an effort to keep his voice calm. "This field is a live minefield."

My face must have registered my confusion. I had been told the field was safe, clear of mines. What was he saying?

"We've taken a wrong turn. We are walking through a live minefield."

My heart leaped to my mouth. Down the hill, my flaxen-haired daughter looked on from the window of the van. Her kerchief bright in the sun, Kyleigh smiled, unaware that anything had gone wrong. Every cell in my body screamed, "Run to her! Run!" But doing that might kill me.

"Walk slowly," Majetić said, urging me to focus. "Step by step, retrace your footsteps exactly. Here, give me your hand."

I followed his instructions, though my mind was racing. How had I gotten myself into this? What kind of mother was I to bring my only daughter to the war-torn fields of Croatia on her thirteenth birthday?

And for what? To let her see me get blown up? Was the risk really worth it? Why dedicate my life to this?

A series of miracles had brought me here, I thought. Surely, a miracle could lead me home. Willing myself to take deep breaths, I repeated a simple prayer: "Faith, not fear." Eyes on Kyleigh, I twisted my body around and took Majetić's hand. Ever so gently, my life flashing before my eyes, we retraced the steps we had taken into the minefield. We made it out, shaken but alive.

To help me recover from the ordeal, the following day, our driver, Rocky, took us to a remote pond where we celebrated Mother's Day with a picnic. Croatia is a beautiful country, and we spent the afternoon admiring the countryside, making crowns of flowers, recovering from the previous day, and marveling at how such beauty could exist side by side with such darkness. It was calming to spend quality time with my teenage daughter and know that we were doing what we could for mothers and children who suffered the perils of landmines. Despite the horror of the day before, it was the best Mother's Day ever.

I had always dreamed of visiting Medjugorje, the town in Bosnia-Herzegovina that has been a place of Catholic pilgrimage ever since the Virgin Mary appeared to local children in 1981. "Peace, peace and only peace," were the words imparted to the children on June 25, 1981. Those were the same words that had come to me in a dream as a kindergarten child on the same evening that John F. Kennedy had been assassinated, and they were a part of what inspired me to overcome many obstacles and start Roots of Peace.

Now, accompanied by Karen Gonzalez, a reporter from the *San Francisco Chronicle*, my dream was about to come true. Kyleigh understood my devotion to Mary and joined me on the pilgrimage.

Our driver from Dubrovnik to Mostar, who had lived through the war, shared his memories as we drove, speaking vividly about the atrocities he had witnessed. He was not an exception in this regard. Many of the people we met were eager to purge themselves of their tragic memories by recounting them to strangers.

As we drove from the border of Croatia into Bosnia-Herzegovina, we were stopped by four armed guards in the remote high mountain region. These stern men, smelling of alcohol, pointed guns at us and ordered us to get out of the car immediately. Just then, for a very distinct moment, I had the clear and simple knowledge that my survival and the survival of my daughter were at stake as we stood before these people. I pray that you never experience that terrifying feeling. Not a word was spoken, but the animal instinct of protecting my young poured through my veins—and in my fear, I felt a primal power like never before. I hoped I was also exuding it.

The men examined our American passports. Words were exchanged in a local dialect as they lit cigarettes and eyed all three of us women like we were wild dogs. They encircled us threateningly; it was as if the rage and aggression of the war had hit a boiling point in their minds, and they didn't have anything to lose.

I had to act. Grasping multiple newspapers that depicted our delegation in the area, I shook them in their faces with conviction, warning that important people would be looking for my safe arrival in Mostar—beyond the border. I would have said or done anything to get us to safety. After what seemed like an eternity, they waved us on.

It was a sobering moment, to say the least. Even past the border, silent and tense moments ensued. I simply could not let my daughter see how relieved I was—how exposed we had been just moments before. As our taxi descended the mountain road, farther and farther from the crisis we'd averted, I clutched my daughter as if it was the first and last time I ever would; she was like salve to my shaken soul.

We finally arrived at Medjugorje. While some of the officials here had tried to protect tourism by claiming that the village had not been affected by the war, bullet holes on the sides of buildings told a different story. The entire region had suffered.

After hours of driving, we arrived at a private family home that had been recommended by the consul-general of Croatia in Los Angeles as a good place to stay during our visit. We decided that we would not talk to our hosts about our mission in Croatia. We were on pilgrimage and didn't want to discuss war or politics.

We settled into our room and, opening my suitcase, I found carefully wrapped grapevines. Then I remembered that Mike Grgich had brought them from California to be planted in the Medari Vineyards. A legendary Napa Valley vintner and a dear friend had trusted me with his precious vines, and I felt a terrible pang of guilt, realizing that in my preoccupation with the children of Dragalić, I had neglected to plant them. How could I have been so careless?

Just then, our hostess walked into my room with an interpreter. She saw me holding the grapevines, then peered into my suitcase and saw the Roots of Peace mines-to-vines media materials. With a suspicious tone to her voice, she asked, "What is that inside your suitcase?"

My face turned red, and my throat tightened. As politely as possible, I handed over our leaflets and press pack. Then, through our interpreter, I explained the story of Mike Grgich—how he was a Croatian man who went to America, became a big success, founded a winery, and then returned to the former Yugoslavia with the intention of planting these special grapevines from his vineyard in California. My hostess examined the grapevines, handed them back, took my printed materials, then turned around and walked out of the room. I was afraid that my carelessness may have placed my daughter in jeopardy. After all, we were in a Bosnian town, and I'd just revealed that we had come from a mission in Croatia, a former enemy of Bosnia.

Moments later, several people came knocking at our door. The hostess escorted me, Karen, and my daughter into the living room, where her relatives were seated on couches and chairs. I shuddered to think what her next words would be. Instead, she surprised me. Through the interpreter, we learned that our hostess had a niece, Vicka, who was one of the children who in 1981 had seen the image of the Blessed Mother in Medjugorje.

"I am deeply touched by your intentions of turning mines to vines," our hostess said. "Would you like to plant Mr. Grgich's grapevines at the foot of the statue of Our Lady on the site where my niece saw her? Please plant your roots of peace."

I was speechless. The site where children had had their vision of the Virgin Mary was considered sacred ground. Our hostess's offer was an extraordinary gesture of appreciation. We discussed the great divide of misunderstanding caused by warfare and shared the beautiful realization that there is so much that binds us together as people of faith.

The next morning, we drove out to the statue of Our Lady and planted Mike's grapevines at her feet. Today, Mike Grgich and I take great pride knowing that his Napa Valley grapevines are flourishing on such a sacred site, watered by the Roots of Peace vision to heal the wounds of war.

While packing for my and Kyleigh's return home in 2000 after planting the grapevines at the feet of the statue of Our Lady, I received a telephone call from Gillian Sorensen, UN assistant secretary-general for external relations, informing me that Kofi Annan had been invited to be a keynote speaker at Stanford University on June 9, 2000.

"Since he has some additional time in Silicon Valley," Gillian said, "he wants to know if you would like to host a Roots of Peace reception with leaders in the technology and wine industries." It was an ideal opportunity to build on our successes to date, and I immediately accepted.

During the long flight back home, I reflected on the many experiences Kyleigh and I had shared on this trip. The visit had created a mother-daughter bond I sensed neither of us would ever forget. The trip was a rite of passage, and her isolated bubble was broken forever. While other Marin County girls sought the latest pair of designer jeans, she would never forget the young girls of Croatia who yearned for hand-me-downs and jeans wide enough to fit a prosthetic leg. High fashion was destined to take on an entirely different meaning in Kyleigh's life as she learned the importance of obtaining a global education. While there were many challenges along the way, the risk was worth the reward.

The June 7 event in Silicon Valley was only three weeks away, so while Kyleigh slept, I jotted down the names of guests to be invited.

We began mailing formal invitations soon after our return, and the responses were encouraging. Lew Platt, former CEO of Hewlett-Packard, agreed to attend. His new position was CEO of Kendall-Jackson Vineyard Estates, and he clearly understood the business perspective of mines to vines. Many other Silicon Valley leaders responded, as did vintners from Dry Creek Winery and other Sonoma Valley friends of Judy Jordan of J Vineyards and Winery. Once again, our intrepid supporter Jim Lawrence from PM/WRA agreed to attend. So did the former Canadian prime minister, Kim Campbell, whom I had met in Ottawa in 1997, and

Bobby Muller, who had funded my initial launch with Nane Annan, also sent in his acceptance to attend.

The day of the event arrived, and just hours before the scheduled start, I received a call from Gillian warning me that Kofi Annan might need to cancel, as President Hafez al-Assad of Syria had just died of a heart attack, and the secretary-general needed to fly to Syria at once. However, Gillian, a woman of her word, true friend, and ally to Roots of Peace, spoke with the UN secretary-general and convinced him to take a later flight.

Annan attended our event, delivered a moving speech in support of our Roots of Peace mines-to-vines initiative, then left immediately for the Middle East. "You have turned seeds of destruction into seeds of life," he said, "and you have shown the whole world that a partnership backed up by persistence can make a real difference." The event garnered a great deal of attention that in turn led to more support for Roots of Peace. Leaders from Silicon Valley, Sonoma Valley, Napa Valley, and the Wine Institute offered to host a one-day retreat at J Vineyards and Winery to develop a formal business plan for Roots of Peace.

One by one, each piece of the puzzle locked into another, until a picture began to emerge of the possible future of Roots of Peace. The stakes were high: Lives—many of them young lives—hung in the balance. The need was immediate: Deadly landmine explosions happened every single day. And the cause was beneficial for all who took part: Positive press and goodwill followed Roots of Peace wherever we went.

As a result, the Roots of Peace momentum grew rapidly. In August 2000, Hewlett-Packard Foundation provided us with a $40,000 grant to further develop the business plan discussed at the J Vineyards and

Winery retreat, and for a full week, two experts followed me to meetings at the United Nations and various offices of the State Department. The experts asked questions about the project's long-term vision and even came with me to Mass at St. Rose Church in Washington, DC, to better understand how my efforts were spiritually grounded. Of all the points we covered, my phrase "the economics of peace" was the one that resonated with them most: a concise description of raising funds to hire demining companies to clear fields of deadly mines, then training farmers to implement productive, modern farming techniques.

Another piece fell into place when, while flying to New York City, Michael Jacobs, creative director at the global marketing and technology agency Digitas, saw a small article printed in *Newsweek* magazine featuring our mines-to-vines vision of planting the roots of peace. The article, titled "Mine Sweepers," captured his imagination, and he managed to track me down in the basement of our home in California and scheduled a meeting with his team at our "World Headquarters"—our family dining room table. While I was initially embarrassed to host this talented team at our humble abode, I spoke from my heart, and they were able to see the authenticity of my vision.

After the team spoke with David Kenny, the CEO of Digitas, they ultimately chose Roots of Peace for its pro bono nationwide advertising campaign. The company's innovative creative designer, Heward Jue, drew the grapevine and dove of peace as our logo, and then, suddenly, bright orange billboards at mass transit stops all over the United States featured the new Roots of Peace logo with the backdrop of an orange caution sign with catchy phrases like "Would you walk across the street if you knew it was a minefield?" and "Warning: Jogging may be fatal!" and "Walking to school may result in death or injury."

Their strategy was to bring the concept home to America, as we are blessed to live in a country without landmines. A deep friendship grew between me and the entire Digitas advertising team that created the first website for Roots of Peace, led by Jodi Manning. The company's technical director, Tom Tully, even joined our board of directors and remained in the position for nearly two decades.

As a result of this national outreach, David Finn, CEO of the Ruder Finn advertising agency, and his daughter Dena Merriam also offered their pro bono services, and the vision to plant the roots of peace was truly off and running!

As more and more pieces fell into place, old friends continued to support us. Mike Grgich was so deeply touched by his visit to the minefields of his beloved Croatian homeland that he sponsored a Roots of Peace fundraiser at the Domaine Chandon Winery on the occasion of the twenty-fifth anniversary of the Paris Tasting, the 1976 competition between French and Californian wines that had placed Napa Valley on the map. Attendees at Mike's fundraiser included many celebrity vintners, and the event was catered by Thomas Keller, chef of the renowned restaurant French Laundry. Also in attendance were Bob Hurley and other legendary chefs. There was a large silent auction with contributions from more than twenty-five Napa Valley wineries, and the evening raised $66,000, matched by the State Department and the International Trust Fund for Demining and Mine Victims' Assistance. In all, we raised $249,000 for the demining campaign in Croatia.

The Paul Harris Award, named after the cofounder of Rotary International and honoring individuals for their service activities, was later presented to Mike Grgich by the Rotary Club of San Rafael for his leadership role in our Roots of Peace initiative. In addition, over the years, the Rotary Club of San Francisco sent two delegations to Croatia led by current and former chapter presidents John Hoch and Jim Patrick, respectively. Their presence in Croatia, and their courage when it came to walking through the minefields, lent credibility to our organization for those who were concerned how their dollars were being spent in war-torn lands.

Dr. Dijana Pleština, the wife of Croatia's prime minister, was impressed by what she knew of our mission and flew from Zagreb to attend. She and her husband invited Roots of Peace back to Croatia to select additional sites for transforming mines to vines, and I accepted, but on one condition: The trip could not be scheduled until fall at the earliest. I had spent too much time away from my family.

During the summer of 2000, my family and I traveled to our mountain cabin built by my grandfather during the 1930s at Wrights Lake in the Desolation Wilderness, near Lake Tahoe. The cabin had no electricity, plumbing, or hot water, and the bathroom was an outhouse by the creek, but we were together, and that made the place heaven. A canoe, a kayak, wildflowers, and waterfalls brought welcome relief from the tension of Croatian minefields, and the alpine surroundings, at an elevation of 7,000 feet, allowed me to reflect on the beauty of nature. There was no service in the area for landline phones or mobile devices at the time, so my mind was able to take a short break as we hiked the mountains.

For the briefest time, a sense of normalcy had returned to the Kühn household.

CHAPTER FOUR

THIRD MISSION
TO CROATIA

We Will Never Forget

Wheresoever you go,
go with all your heart.

—Confucius

In August 2001, I made a third visit to Croatia, this time with my oldest son, Brooks. I described the trip for him as a rite of passage after his graduation from Marin Catholic High School and before his first year at the University of California, Santa Barbara. His sister, Kyleigh, said her trip to Croatia had been a significant episode in her life, and now I wanted Brooks to have a similar experience working with me in the minefields of the Balkans. Nothing, I told him, could be more effective for developing the most important tools for life such as compassion and love for our fellow human beings. He was a teenager, and he listened as best he could.

"OK, Mom, OK," he said.

Soon after our inconclusive mother-son talk, I heard from 1997 Nobel Peace Prize recipient Jody Williams, who agreed to fly with us as part of our Roots of Peace delegation. Since our initial meeting at the signing of the Anti-Personnel Mine Ban Treaty in Ottawa, Jody had joined our board of directors. She is a woman who walks the talk, and her words of wisdom would be inspiring to my son: "I believe that worrying about the problems plaguing our planet without taking steps to confront them is absolutely irrelevant. The only thing that changes the world is taking action."

What a team, I thought: A mother, a son, and a Nobel Peace Prize winner turning ideas into action! We boarded our flight later that month.

In Croatia, we witnessed the fruits of what Roots of Peace had begun over the past couple of years. In Dragalić, the mayor greeted us with a smile that was brighter than ever, although he had visibly aged as a result of the hardships of life in his village. We inspected the vineyards and found that the local farmers had done extensive planting after our land-mine removal. In the surrounding area, many homes had been repaired. The local school now featured a fully equipped kitchen that provided students with fresh, warm meals. In most cases, it was the Croatian schoolchildren's only warm meal of the day. The students had planted a garden in honor of Roots of Peace, where they grew fresh vegetables.

I watched with interest as a few of the children took my son aside and regaled him with stories about our delegation's earlier visits to Dragalić. Together, they picked the fresh fruits grown on former minefields and made their own version of stone soup (named after a popular folktale), and the taste of peace was sweet.

It seemed that everyone—even in remote areas of Croatia—knew that Jody Williams was a Nobel Prize recipient. Media and press followed us everywhere we went, and the return of Roots of Peace was reported nationwide. Jody shared her passion for peace with the reporters, saying, "What we need today is people getting up and taking action to reclaim the meaning of peace. It's hard work every single day." With tireless footsteps, we continued our journey.

Next, we traveled to Vukovar, where I pointed out to my son the giant water tank riddled with bullet holes that villagers had preserved as a reminder of what war had done to their ancestral village. There were some encouraging signs that Vukovar was coming back to life, and, as in Dragalić, many homes had been rebuilt, but much of the village remained in ruins.

Later that day, Brooks and I decided to take a break to rest and reflect. Looking out over the majestic Danube River, set against the ruins of battle, we sat and pondered the meaning of war and the need for healing in this world. It was a rare mother-and-son moment. We spoke of his upcoming plans to attend UC Santa Barbara: registering for classes and setting up his dormitory room (and the importance of getting along with roommates). As I looked at his profile reflecting on the edge of the river, I pondered what the future might hold for a fine young man as he stands on the edge of the global stage. I remembered the courage this young boy had shown at five years old while watching his mother struggle with a shocking diagnosis of cancer. Brooks was strong, brilliant, and determined, and he had, most important, learned compassion. Each morning, when all my children woke, I would greet them softly with the words "Rise to the stars of your greater destiny!" Now, he was on the precipice of seeking his own destiny.

Suddenly, two Croatian boys wearing soccer jerseys appeared in the distance, kicking a soccer ball back and forth along the pathway. The afternoon sun was setting, and the brilliant orange and red colors of the sky made a surreal backdrop to the two teenage boys and their ball. Sounds of laughter emerged as they came closer. But then the ball was kicked too hard, and it bounced straight in our direction. Brooks intuitively ran to catch the ball before it could roll into the river.

"Here's your ball, guys!" gasped my breathless son.

"*Hvala!*" exclaimed the boys. After saying "Thank you" in Croatian, they paused.

"Hey, are you American?" the boys asked in unison. "What are you doing in Vukovar?"

A conversation ensued as the two boys, who were younger than Brooks, explained that they were brothers who had been studying English in their local school. Given that few American tourists traveled through war zones, they told him they took every opportunity to practice their language with foreigners. Their conversation continued in English, and I listened.

After their introductions were made, they started to talk about the serious nature of the war and the importance of the international community stepping in and helping to rebuild their homes. Over 154,000 homes had been destroyed in Vukovar when the Serbian forces came over the Danube River only a few years earlier. They pointed to the destroyed water tower in the distance. When they asked Brooks what he was doing in Vukovar, he told them that his mother had come up with an idea four years earlier to help remove landmines and plant vineyards in war-torn lands.

As they both reached down to pull up the legs of their sweatpants, they casually told Brooks that they were landmine victims and showed him their prostheses. As I listened in disbelief, they told him how they had been collecting wood in the forest with their father to keep the family warm during the winter. Suddenly, a landmine blast blew their collection of wood into the air, and the two boys were left lying on the ground, each missing a leg. Neighbors had heard the noise, and brave locals quickly made a pathway to retrieve the boys as they lay in their own blood, screaming for their mother. During the war, there were no official deminers, so the locals had needed to learn how to remove landmines by themselves. Their father was never found; like the wood, he was blown into splinters.

I watched my son's reaction to this story, and I realized that he was destined to become a healer. This moment was one of the many seeds planted in Brooks's heart. Years later, these seeds of compassion would grow, and he eventually became Brooks Kühn, MD, working in the intensive care unit at the UC Davis Medical Center.

When we returned to Zagreb, the president of Croatia, Stjepan Mesić, invited us to visit the presidential palace. From the windows of this historic building, we looked out onto a breathtaking view of the city. Croatian media were there when the president honored our efforts to turn mines to vines in his great country and presented my son Brooks with a medal in recognition of his participation.

When the day came for us to return to visit the former minefields, we arrived at the local airport for our trip to Dubrovnik. As we walked toward the gate, stern Croatian security guards with guns ordered us to go in the opposite direction. I tried to explain that this was the way to our Croatia Airlines flight and that we could not delay our arrival in Dubrovnik for the connecting flight home. Again, they motioned with their guns to steer us to another location on the opposite side of the airport. They spoke no English, and we had no choice but to do as we were told, not knowing where we were going.

We passed through a door that opened onto the tarmac, and there, looming in front of us, was the president's private jet. The pilot came forward and explained that Mesić had ordered the plane for us, as he wanted us to travel with the utmost safety. "It is his way of thanking you for your good work in his beloved country," he said. We boarded the aircraft, which featured white marble tables and plush cushioned seats. The aircraft lifted off, and we were airborne on the most comfortable flight of our lives—and that was the moment when Brooks acknowledged that maybe coming with me hadn't been such a bad choice after all.

"Mom, you're too cool" was, I think, the way he put it.

From the air, I looked out over the vast country below and remembered that much of Croatia was still infested with landmines and that those of us on that flight had much more work to do, here and elsewhere.

The flight arrived in Dubrovnik, where we would spend two days before flying home. We spent the first day visiting the war museum. The walls displayed historic portraits of young men, many of them Brooks's age, who had taken up guns and marched with their fathers to defend their city. Many had been killed in battle, but their sacrifices had paved the way for the nation's independence.

Dijana Pleština joined us and arranged for a military helicopter to show us the Dalmatian coast—a rare opportunity to fly low over hundreds of islands lining the Adriatic Sea and take in the breathtaking view through the helicopter's open doors. It landed in a field in Bibinje, a wine-growing region Mike Grgich had selected for our project, and farmers and their families were there to greet us. We walked to the edge of a vineyard that featured a red sign written in Croatian: "Warning: Landmines. Do not walk." It was troubling, seeing vineyards ripe with fruit, yet knowing that any attempt to harvest them could result in the loss of a limb or death. Many farmers had taken this risk, and they were there in large numbers, standing at the edge of the field. Their missing limbs attested to the sad reality of war.

The next day, we flew home.

As our plane approached New York City on a clear September morning, I pointed to the glistening World Trade Center's twin towers rising in the distance and reminded Brooks of one of the McNear family mottos: "Reach for the sky."

We arrived at John F. Kennedy International Airport in New York City on September 9 and, a few hours later, boarded our flight to San Francisco. The wheels went up, and I thought how wonderful it was to be back in the safety of our own country, where children never had to endure the devastations of war. Despite the jet lag, I was happy to return to a life of normalcy and just be a mom again. The plane was relatively empty, so we stretched out and slept. Terrible nightmares of bloodshed with thousands of suffering souls filled my mind as I flew on this United Airlines flight back home.

Looking back, it was a foreshadowing of the events to come just two days later.

We arrived in San Francisco that evening, and by the following morning, we were comfortably ensconced back home, delighted to again be enjoying the view of San Francisco Bay from our living room window.

The next morning, Gary prepared to go off to work, and at 7 A.M., I turned on the television while preparing lunches for my children's first day back at school. Live broadcasts of the attacks on the Twin Towers had taken over every channel. I held my children tightly. The moment was doubly horrifying because my son and I had just arrived home from a war zone and had seen what fanaticism could do. Like everyone else, we feared that there might be a follow-up attack on the West Coast. Rumors were flying as we sat there terrified that San Francisco International Airport or the Golden Gate Bridge could be next.

From our basement, clatter from the fax machine filtered up the stairs. Messages were pouring in from our friends in Croatia. The relationship had been turned upside down, and they were now the ones consoling us. It was so strange. We had been together only a few days before, celebrating the work of Roots of Peace, never imagining that our own country would resemble war-ravaged Vukovar.

The phone rang. It was a Glenwood neighbor calling to tell me that our friend Lauren Grandcolas had been on board United Airlines Flight 93. Lauren had been in New Jersey attending her grandmother's funeral when she received word from her doctor that she was pregnant with her first child. She had booked a seat on Flight 93—an earlier flight than originally planned—in order to share the good news with her husband, Jack, as quickly as possible and in person. She and her unborn child were killed when her plane crashed into the fields of Pennsylvania.

All night, I tossed and turned. War had come to our own shores, and I wondered, "Where *wasn't* war?" I had seen the heartbreak and suffering it caused abroad. I had now seen it in my very own country. I had seen it in the actions of people who didn't know better. I had felt the fear of it in my own heart. It was enormous, but it also seemed granular, somehow.

Was there a war inside many humans who could do such evil things? Was my work doing any good? It was easy to spin out, so I did what I always do when I don't know what to do: I prayed. I pleaded with God for some sign that at this moment, the most catastrophic in the recent history of our nation, he really did want me to continue trying to build peace around the world, one safe footstep at a time. As I closed my eyes on that fateful day, the words of Proverbs 3:5 echoed in my mind, as softly whispered to me by my Granny McNear:

Trust in the Lord
With all thy heart,
And lean not on thy own understanding.
In all thy ways trust in him,
And he shall direct thy path.

CHAPTER FIVE

BACK TO THE GARDEN

Darkness cannot drive out darkness; only light can do that.
Hate cannot drive out hate. Only love can do that.

—Martin Luther King Jr.

In the immediate aftermath of 9/11, Americans did not know how far the terrorism would penetrate US soil. Rumors of impending additional attacks were rampant. Still, Gary and I gave our son Brooks our blessings to start college and go forth into the world. With every fiber in my body, I wanted to keep him home, as if by being physically near him, I could keep him safe. Nevertheless, Gary and I had to trust that we'd given him the tools he needed to grow. We drove Brooks down to UC Santa Barbara to register, and we brought our three younger children along, as we dared not be separated at such a time, when acts of terrorism might happen again.

Over the next several months, we watched news reports of the bombing of Afghanistan in Operation Enduring Freedom, a multinational effort led by the United States to drive al-Qaeda and the Taliban from power. It was not only soldiers who were killed in these campaigns; tragically, innocent women and children also perished. From our firsthand observations of the deadly effects of landmines, I had become somewhat hardened to images of war, but who could fail to be moved by scenes of young children killed as collateral damage in the hunt for Osama bin Laden?

In October 2001, President George W. Bush established America's Fund for Afghan Children, appealing to American children to donate just one dollar each for the relief effort. The president's initiative was modeled on the March of Dimes campaign started by Franklin D. Roosevelt's administration: In the 1930s and '40s, every child was asked to donate a dime for the eradication of polio. In 1974, as a sixteen-year-old sophomore at San Rafael High School, I had served as the local youth president for the March of Dimes, and I understood the power of such grassroots efforts.

A few weeks after the attacks, the Kühn family gathered at our kitchen table and discussed the painful statistics concerning the fate of Afghan children. The country ranked number one worldwide in infant mortality. One in four Afghan children did not live to see a fifth birthday. One out of every three was an orphan. Almost half suffered from chronic malnutrition, and millions more faced starvation in the harsh winter months ahead.

Later that evening, we took our family to dinner at the Bamyan Afghan Restaurant, located in San Rafael's Montecito Plaza shopping center. Over the years, the owners, Walid and Nadia, had become our friends. When we arrived, they were visibly shaken by the attacks. We noted that they had scissored the word *Afghan* out of their menus to cover up their heritage. Their three children hovered in the kitchen to avoid drive-by shootings against Muslims, as if their innocent family was somehow personally responsible for the 9/11 catastrophe. Some gesture of support for innocent people such as them was needed, and we proposed to Walid and Nadia that we host a Roots of Peace fundraiser in their restaurant for demining in Afghanistan. They were hesitant, concerned that no one would attend an event in a restaurant run by a Muslim family in Marin County.

Working with friends, we filled the room with over one hundred guests and engaged rock star Dave Jenkins of the band Pablo Cruise to sing "America the Beautiful." As a community, we honored those in Marin County who protected us each day, including the chief of police, the chief of the local fire department, and the mayor. Once again, the Marin Community Foundation stepped forward and underwrote the cost of the event. We auctioned paintings by renowned environmentalist and artist George Sumner depicting the Statue of Liberty reaching toward the heavens, and at the dinner, thousands of dollars were raised to support a mines-to-vines initiative in Afghanistan, a country located on the other side of the world where few—if any—of our guests had ever been. How I should properly distribute those funds in Afghanistan was another big part of the puzzle I had to figure out, but I was confident I could solve the problem.

It was around this time that I received an invitation from US Secretary of State Colin Powell to attend an event coinciding with the anniversary of the signing of the Anti-Personnel Mine Ban Treaty. Despite the disturbing fact that the United States still had not signed the treaty, the PM/WRA office was proud that the United States had generously donated more than any other country for the eradication of landmines, and it was flattering to think that the government saw Roots of Peace as a symbol of that growing movement. I received permission to bring four business friends, and I chose Jim Clerkin, vice president of the Diageo Wine Group; Austin Hills, co-owner of Grgich Hills Estate; Robert B. Chavez, CEO of the fashion brand Hermès of Paris; and Skip Rhodes, vice president for community affairs at Chevron. That company had just merged with Texaco, and the removal of landmines dovetailed with its mandate to demonstrate corporate social responsibility.

In December 2001, when we walked into the delegates' dining room at the State Department, Colin Powell came forward to greet me. Skip Rhodes was sufficiently impressed by the dinner to pledge $30,000 to Roots of Peace for the removal of landmines in Battambang, Cambodia. The legacy of three decades of war had taken a severe toll on the Cambodians. The country has some 40,000 amputees, representing one of the highest rates in the world. The Cambodian Mine Action Center (CMAC) estimates that as many as six million mines and other pieces of unexploded ordnance (UXO) were sown in the soils of Cambodia.

The widespread presence of landmines motivated Roots of Peace to partner with the nongovernmental organization MAG (Mines Advisory Group) to remove the landmines and UXO that haunt the country. The rural population in Cambodia is largely poor and dependent on agriculture for their livelihood, and we could not leave the land fallow. Therefore, we also partnered with the Lutheran World Federation to plant rice after MAG released the land from danger and fear and gave the safe land back to communities so they could feed their families and earn a living.

TOP LEFT: The author, Heidi Kühn, riding a camel in Giza, Egypt, in 1975.

TOP RIGHT: The Kühn family in September 1997 when the mines-to-vines toast began: (clockwise from top) Gary, Tucker, Christian, Heidi, Kyleigh, and Brooks.

ABOVE: Roots of Peace launch at the World Trade Club in San Francisco, April 20, 1998: (clockwise from top left) Congresswoman Nancy Pelosi, Jerry White, Heidi Kühn, Nane Annan, Bobby Muller, and Gail Griffith. Photo courtesy of Christine Torrington.

TOP: Gary and Heidi in the minefields of
Huambo, Angola, where Princess Diana once
walked.

ABOVE: In discussion with Afghan women from
the Shomali Plain about ways to plant the roots of
peace as farmers.

TOP: At the Kyleigh Kühn School in Mir Bacha Kot, Afghanistan.

LEFT: Kyleigh with mine survivor Fawad Afa, in Kabul, Afghanistan, in August 2005.

ABOVE: With Kyleigh and a group of female Afghan students in Bam Saray. Kyleigh raised fifty million pennies to build schools in Afghanistan.

TOP: Meeting with local Afghan leaders at Bagram Air Base: (from left to right) General David Petraeus, General John F. Campbell, Heidi Kühn, and Afghan provincial governors.

ABOVE: With Shamim Jawad presenting fresh pomegranates to President Hamid Karzai at the palace in Kabul, Afghanistan.

BOTTOM LEFT: Plaque featured at the dedication of the Roots of Peace Garden, signed by Adrian Benepe, former Commissioner of the New York City Department of Parks and Recreation.

BOTTOM RIGHT: Inscription on the Isaiah Wall outside the Roots of Peace Garden across from the United Nations Headquarters in New York City.

From a distance, Roots of Peace empowered the Cambodian farmers and cultivated a harvest of hope.

During the spring of 2002, I researched the situation in Afghanistan in preparation for bringing Roots of Peace to that part of the world and discovered that Afghanistan was 80 percent dependent on agriculture, but the vineyards north of Kabul, in the Shomali Plain, had been burned by the Soviet army during its 1979 invasion. If that wasn't bad enough, the Taliban had infested the area with landmines, and an estimated ten million landmines and other UXOs were buried across the country. Once-lush fields of grapevines were now desolate wastelands, the sight of which broke the spirit of the Afghan farmers who had tilled the soil and cultivated the vineyards for countless generations.

Clearly, Afghanistan could use the kind of assistance Roots of Peace had provided in Croatia, but it would be an immense hardship for us to expand into a second country. I didn't want to give up, but how could the project take on more responsibility just now? Finding new sources of funding had become critical.

By September 2002, we were hyperconscious of the one-year anniversary of the 9/11 attacks and the growing importance of our work, but as a businessman, Gary couldn't help noticing that the project's accounting system was rather amateurish. All our receipts were literally stuffed into shoeboxes in the basement of our family home.

"Heidi, sweetheart," he said, "there has to be a more efficient way to keep track of your receipts. Let me take over. This is my specialty. Besides, I've done well enough financially. Now I want to do some good." From that moment on, Gary took over our accounting and kept close tabs on the business side of Roots of Peace while I continued to dream big for peace.

While the children were at school, Gary joined me on the drive to the University of California, Davis, where we met with professionals to research ways of turning mines to vines in Afghanistan. There, we learned of Dr. Harold Olmo, "the Indiana Jones of viticulture," who had ridden on horseback across Afghanistan in the 1940s to gather grape varietals. Knowing there were more than seventy varietals, Olmo created a living library of rootstock when he returned to UC Davis. The viticulture school cultivated the Afghan varietals and over the decades had succeeded in preserving them. Then came the war that destroyed nearly all the Afghan vineyards. Ironically, the only place where Afghan rootstock had been preserved was right there in the heart of California.

When I was informed about this tantalizing bit of botanical lore, the thought occurred to me that there must be some way to restore the ancient vines to their source. A little more research revealed that there were three main varieties indigenous to Afghanistan: Kishmishi, Shindokhani, and Taifi. The more I found out about the glories of Afghanistan's tradition of growing grapes, the more I wanted to return these seeds to where they belonged. It just felt like the right thing to do, an act of peace in a time of war. We also discovered an important qualifier for our work: Afghan farmers never fermented their grapes because of the Muslim cultural ban on wine. Instead, the country's farmers produced fresh table grapes and dried raisins.

As the one-year anniversary of 9/11 approached, I wanted to honor our neighbor Lauren Grandcolas and her unborn child, who had died on Flight 93, by gathering mothers from our Glenwood community at the Kühn family dining room table. Together, we gathered over three thousand daffodil bulbs and wrapped each in white netting, then tied a ribbon with a message on each bulb: "May we all plant the Roots of Peace on Earth." The bulbs were a tribute to the lives lost to violence as we sought to replace seeds of terror with seeds of hope. That afternoon, a white dove flew in and landed on the pile of bulbs outside our window. Doves are not indigenous to our part of the country, and my daughter, Kyleigh, sat watching the dove for nearly an hour. It felt like a symbol of the Holy Spirit and a blessing for our heartfelt intentions.

We carefully packed the bulbs and sent them to St. Bartholomew's Church in New York City. FedEx was now familiar with our new charity and offered to fly the bulbs without charge. Katie Taraban, a classmate of my son Brooks, volunteered during the summer to help me achieve my vision with "flower power." Together, we coordinated the shipment.

At the conclusion of a moving interfaith service for the victims of the 9/11 tragedy, the children placed the bulbs into the hands of family members who had lost loved ones. Daffodils represent "the chalice of life," which stretches toward heaven and holds up the spirit. My youngest son, Christian, then six years old, teared up as he joined the children of New York City in this gesture of love.

After the ceremony, we knelt in the church and renewed our vow to help the families of Afghanistan. I bowed my head, as I had no idea how this dream was to be fulfilled.

Later that month, I turned to my friend Erika Hills, co-owner of Grgich Hills Estate, and asked whether she might host another fundraiser luncheon for Roots of Peace at her La Encantada estate in the Napa Valley, and she readily agreed. Dori Bonn, a former flight attendant for Pan Am and a close friend, began to arrange details for the event. The women of the vine were now blending borders for peace. Dede Wilsey, a San Francisco philanthropist, generously donated $100,000, and our important work in Croatia continued to be funded while I pursued my dream for Afghanistan.

At the luncheon, I was seated next to a lovely woman who seemed genuinely interested in our campaign. Introducing herself as Diane Miller, the owner of Silverado Vineyards, she asked me for specific details about Roots of Peace and was very persistent and inquisitive. Fascinated by the concept of turning mines to vines, she suggested we get together the following week.

Several days later, Diane and I met and spoke in detail about growing grapes in Afghanistan. She offered to volunteer at our Roots of Peace headquarters, so I invited her to join me in the basement of our family home to sort papers and organize files. Week after week, she drove from Napa to help out. One day, she invited me for lunch at Il Davide in San Rafael to take a break from our daily activities, and she asked me why I had sacrificed so much on behalf of children I'd never met. At first, she listened carefully and didn't say much. Then, without warning, she pounded the table with her fist.

"That's it!" she said. "Somebody needs to do this."

Then she took out her checkbook, wrote a check, and handed it to me, saying, "Here's a Mickey to help remove some landmines and plant grapevines."

I had no idea what she meant by "a Mickey," but I looked at the check and gulped to find it was for $200,000, the largest check I'd ever seen.

"You remind me of my dad," Diane said. "He knew a thing or two about turning a vision into a reality."

"Who was your dad?" I asked innocently.

"Walt Disney," she said, as casually as if she was asking me to pass the salt. And like that, Roots of Peace was funded for a mines-to-vines campaign in Afghanistan. I love telling that story whenever anyone asks me why I'm such a believer in divine intervention, miracles, and magical moments.

Over the next few months of 2002, Diane often joined me in the basement of our home to help with office work. She said the basement setup reminded her of the garage where her dad had started the Disney empire. Apparently, Walt Disney was told no by more than 300 naysayers before his designs for Mickey Mouse were taken seriously.

"Don't mind how often people say no," she said. "The time will come when Roots of Peace will be well established. For now, the greatest gift of all is patience."

Some of these early meetings included taping giant pieces of white paper to our living room wall and writing ideas on them with colored markers. Gary added ideas drawing upon his IBM business acumen, and Diane reveled in the excitement of seeing new concepts come to life before her eyes. She said it reminded her of the storyboard meetings her father used to conduct.

Together, we determined that the first step in bringing Roots of Peace to Afghanistan would be to partner with the right agencies already there. Two were most important: the HALO Trust, the anti-mines organization Princess Diana had championed, and the United Nations Mine Action Service (UNMAS). Because we already had strong connections with the UN, we decided it would be best to partner with Martin Barber, director of UNMAS, for the landmine-removal stage. Martin, a stately gentleman, served as our strong advocate at the UN, along with Gillian Sorensen, assistant secretary-general to Kofi Annan.

Then Gary offered a reality check and insisted that he should make a preliminary trip to Afghanistan to establish our business operations. The dangers of Afghanistan in the aftermath of 9/11 came to mind, and I felt a cold chill just thinking about the Taliban and what they were capable of doing to Americans. The vision of turning mines to vines always felt so noble and selfless, but now my husband was reminding me how difficult it was to effect change in the real world, especially in a tribal culture as old as Afghanistan's. The Roots of Peace dream was proving to be a great risk to my family, yet I couldn't really argue with him. He was right. We had to establish a base and build trust on the ground.

To help Gary on this trip, I contacted Larry N. Vanderhoef, chancellor of UC Davis, to enlist the support of its highly respected College of Agriculture and Environmental Sciences. We were actually driving on the highway past UC Davis when I recalled the $35 million gift from Robert and Margrit Mondavi to benefit the Robert Mondavi Institute for Wine and Food Science and the Robert and Margrit Mondavi Center for the Performing Arts. This generous gift, presented shortly after 9/11, was the largest private contribution to UC Davis—in fact, it was one of the largest gifts in the history of the University of California system.

Gary challenged me to call the school, as we were traveling with Nadia Tarzi-Saccardi, founder of the Association for the Protection of Afghan Archaeology (APAA) and daughter of renowned Afghan archaeologist Dr. Zemaryalai Tarzi. Nadia was another Marin County mother dedicated to helping us navigate our entrance to Kabul, and she was escorting us on a visit to meet a group of Afghan Americans living in Sacramento.

So I flipped open my mobile phone and placed the call. Gary smirked as if in disbelief. Then, as I explained our passion, UC Davis's chancellor came on the line and connected me to Patrick Brown, director of international programs at the College of Agriculture and Environmental Sciences at UC Davis. Two weeks later, Patrick and Gary were on the plane to Kabul, and I held my breath, knowing they were flying into a simmering war zone. Where had my intrepid footsteps taken me and my family? This was no joke, and I cringed when signing the form as CEO of Roots of Peace to request the visa that would allow them access to Afghanistan as civilians.

My youngest son, Christian, was now eight years old, and I dropped him off at Glenwood Elementary School as Tucker and Kyleigh carpooled to Marin Catholic High School. As we drove in silence over the Golden Gate Bridge, my heart beat loudly as I chauffeured my beloved husband, Gary, to San Francisco International Airport to board the plane. What would I tell my children if something went wrong? Yet Gary assured me that this was his decision too, and that I must trust his footsteps, as I trust in the Lord.

Gary and Patrick flew from San Francisco to London, arriving in time for lunch at the airport the following day. Already severely jet lagged, they boarded a second flight from London to Dubai. This would be Gary's first visit to an Arab nation, and it had him worried. Like most Americans, his impression of Afghanistan came from popular media reports: a place uncompromisingly chauvinistic and disdainful of women, especially a determined and aggressive woman like me. What would happen to me if I ever decided to fly to such a place? Gary was taking intrepid footsteps on my behalf.

This was at a time when air travel had changed forever, first in the aftermath of 9/11 and then again in 2002 because of Richard Reid, the

Shoe Bomber, a British terrorist who had attempted to detonate an explosive device packed into his shoes while on an American Airlines flight. I thought about him every time I was obliged to walk barefoot through airport security.

The connecting flight from Dubai to Kabul took two and a half hours, flying over Iran, then southern Afghanistan. As they neared Kabul, the flight attendants handed out customs forms for passengers to fill out. It turned out that many of the Afghan passengers were illiterate, and after helping the two people seated on either side of him complete their forms, Gary looked down the aisle: Passengers had seen him lending a hand and had formed a line. He ended up helping an additional fifty passengers before he disembarked.

The plane taxied up to the terminal. Most of the metal letters on the side of the arrivals building had been shot off, but he could make out the remains of "Kabul International" hanging on the terminal wall. The tarmac was scorched black. Two MiGs parked to the right of their plane had taken direct missile hits. Almost every aircraft on the runway showed similar damage, and few seemed airworthy. Missile strikes had made sure of that.

Gary joined a mass of robed men heading for the arrivals terminal and made his way down a gloomy corridor—there were few lights still functioning in the airport—and two hours later, he cleared passport control and entered the Afghan equivalent of baggage claim: a half-block-long room with bags thrown together in a high mound. Baggage in the airport of war-torn Kabul was not baggage as we usually conceive of it, with clothing neatly packed into sturdy suitcases with wheels, but mostly bundles of belongings tied up in cloth and secured with lengths of rope. Dozens of men were climbing over this cloth mountain, looking for their bundles. Under their weight, the pile tumbled down, exposing Gary's Western luggage, which had been buried near the bottom.

Gary's only connection in Afghanistan was Duane Goodno, who guided them while waving an ID badge at any uniformed person who dared to challenge him. Duane, an ex-military guy who had run logistics for a helicopter squadron in Europe, was now in Kabul in his second career, running vocational training programs for women. Pushing his way through the airport like he owned the place, he hurried Gary to his car waiting outside the terminal, engine running. His Afghan driver, not missing a beat, moved them quickly out of the airport and headed for town. Clearly, it was a routine they had executed before.

The road was in terrible shape, and the driver cut back and forth to avoid potholes. Gary passed donkey carts, hand-pulled wagons laden with produce, and an occasional white UN vehicle. He saw ordinary men patrolling the sidewalks carrying every imaginable type of weapon, from antique muskets to modern AK-47s. There were no local police on patrol, mostly soldiers from NATO's International Security Assistance Force, who moved through town in armored caravans with .50-caliber machine guns locked and loaded. He passed eight-wheeled armored personnel carriers and what looked like surplus World War II jeeps. During that trip, the only American military presence they saw was not on the ground but in the sky: twin-engine heavy-lift Chinook helicopters heading out in the evening on night missions.

The fifteen-minute trip from the airport to their hotel felt like an eternity. Gary had been to developing countries before, but this place was stuck so far back in time that, except for some of the vehicles, it was hard to tell what century you were in. The devastation of the city was also readily apparent. If you wanted to see the consequences of war, you did not have to look far. In the Shahr-e Naw neighborhood of northwest Kabul, most of the buildings were still standing, but almost every wall was riddled with bullet holes. Trees had been destroyed, and the whole area was littered with rubble. None of the residents had water or electricity or functioning sewage treatment.

Their hotel, the Gandamack Lodge, wasn't so bad, but it was ironic on a couple of counts. First, the place had earned a nickname, "Last Stand at Gandamack," referring to the disastrous withdrawal of the British from Kabul in 1842. Years later, I would take the path those British colonists traveled as they attempted to escape the Afghans harassing them through rough terrain tailor-made for ambushes and snipers. The second count was that Gandamack Lodge was where one of Osama bin Laden's wives had taken up residence after the 9/11 disaster.

It was only 4 P.M., but Afghanistan time is a half-day ahead of California, and jet lag was slamming Gary hard. He collapsed on the hotel bed, only to wake up fully dressed at 3 A.M. The hotel generator was down for the night, so he worked on his computer until the battery ran out of power, then lay in bed until the sun came up.

He was the first to show up in the hotel dining room for breakfast that morning. Other expats drifted in and sat at a long communal table, mostly British and American journalists fresh from covering recent elections in East Timor.

Later that morning, he set out with his host, Duane, and their translator Mohammad Sharif Osmani for the Shomali Plain, north of Kabul, to meet representatives from the HALO Trust, our demining partner, and from there to inspect the main grape-production region of the country. As they drove out of the central part of Kabul, paved streets gave way to dirt roads. Their driver's nickname was Ziggy, so called because he made a habit of weaving constantly back and forth around potholes in the road. They sped up a bit but soon came to a checkpoint, the first of many unauthorized roadblocks set up for scamming money from drivers. Sharif spoke for them, telling the soldiers why they were there and that they had no money to give them. Ten yards away, another soldier pointed an intimidating anti-aircraft gun at them. Gary politely suggested to Sharif that maybe they could spare a few dollars, but Sharif held his ground and with a firm voice continued to describe their noble purpose. To everyone's huge relief, the soldiers relented and allowed them to pass.

As harrowing as the moment had been for Gary, it provided an important insight into the mission that Roots of Peace had set for itself: Insurgents, rogue soldiers, even terrorists have to feed their families and can see the logic in allowing us to improve their farmlands. Many illegal checkpoints later, Gary came to trust Sharif's negotiating skills implicitly.

As they drove north, signs of the Afghan-Russian and Taliban-Massoud conflicts littered the roadside. Blown-up tanks and armored personnel carriers (APCs) lay where they had been hit by rockets. Many destitute Afghans lived by selling scrap from abandoned vehicles, but it was clear that these vehicles were untouched. Gary asked Duane about them and learned why: Looking closely, you could see that the tanks and APCs had been booby-trapped.

The group arrived at HALO's tent city, where, after officials greeted them, they suited up in flak jackets and helmets and joined the HALO mine-clearance teams on a tour of the mine-infested area. The fighting had ended there three years before, but because of the heavy mining, no one dared enter the surrounding fields. According to our guide, so far, at least one person every day that year had died from landmines in Afghanistan. The team leader led them down a one-meter-wide path that had been cleared of mines. The battles had left a trail of dead bodies, and as HALO deminers cleared the area, they were able to reach fallen soldiers and give them proper burials.

For years, civil war had left the local population without usable farmland. The land was still fertile, but landmines had made planting and harvesting impossible, and the previous year had brought a drought that exacerbated the farmers' plight. Fields that for generations had yielded crops to feed villagers now lay parched and barren. Gary spoke with several people who described how their families survived by eating grass and weeds. The United Nations High Commissioner for Refugees had done what it could to help by erecting tent cities in clusters throughout the Shomali Plain, but tents did nothing to alleviate perpetual gnawing hunger.

The primary challenge was to evaluate the HALO Trust's plans for mine clearance. After touring the minefield, Gary recommended they shift their priorities. Until now, their approach had been to first demine villages, but they had ignored farms and irrigation canals. This allowed Afghans to return home but did nothing to relieve their hunger, and the result was that farmers entered their mined vineyards to resume working and died. Since famine was the most urgent emergency, we recommended that the initial effort be to clear mines from the canals so that water could reach the land. The HALO staff saw the logic in this thinking, and we settled on a rollout that would start with the region's main canals and afterward focus on the smaller canals. Roots of Peace pledged $200,000 from Diane Disney Miller's generous gift, entrusted to UNMAS, that would cover three teams over a two-year period.

Gary headed back to his hotel in Kabul before sunset; Sharif had explained that it would not be good to get caught out of town after dark. "Highway robbers are everywhere," he said. When I was a girl, I'd read the term "highway robbers" in short stories and novels. Until Gary relayed this story, it never occurred to me that they might really exist. The three men arrived at the hotel, exhausted, covered with dust, and thoughtful about the enormity of the work ahead.

The next morning, Gary returned to the Shomali Plain to meet with local grape farmers and described for them the mission of Roots of Peace and our goal of transforming mines to vines. Americans in this remote area of the country stood out, and within minutes they were surrounded by dozens of local farmers and their families.

This was in September, only one month away from harvest time. For most of these people, the older generation of farmers in their families had been killed during the years of fighting, and now it was the sons and grandsons who worked the land. Here was a generation following in the footsteps of their ancestors, using techniques of farming dating back a thousand years. Over multiple discussions, translated back and forth, and after drinking way too much tea, they created a list of steps needed to implement modern techniques and achieve more efficient, profitable harvests. It was another long, dry day, but much was accomplished, and Gary and his companions returned to their hotel satisfied.

In discussions with the farmers, it was clear that they would be reluctant to trust outsiders—especially Americans. Roots of Peace was an unknown entity there, and their families were barely surviving. Any misstep would prove fatal to some members of the family. So Gary and Patrick agreed to focus their efforts on activities that would be successful and show rapid positive results. We had to gain some credibility quickly;

otherwise, our efforts would stall. There were other organizations talking to the farmers, but many of them were heavy on promises and absent on delivery. With the threat of termination, Gary made his team pledge never to make promises—just deliver results.

Patrick made a list of forty-four problems facing the Afghan farmers. The grape growers were in terrible shape. The last knowledgeable farmers to tend these vineyards had either died in the fighting or had left the country. We were dealing with their sons, who were too young to receive their fathers' training. Gary and Patrick focused on six basic needs for the grape growers and began to push that focus.

Gary traveled to Kabul many times by himself that year. Each time, I'd be home in California, berating myself for having agreed to let him do so. Two of our children were attending Marin Catholic High School, and our youngest son was in Glenwood Elementary School in San Rafael; I bridled my feelings in Marin County, where very few mothers knew what it was like to send their husbands to a war zone. Few military families resided in our affluent community, and there were no support groups. There were days when it was hard to keep it all together. Whispers spread in the neighborhood, "Who was this mother who could possibly think she might have an impact on Afghanistan? Does she understand the risks to her family?" When Gary finally returned from his last trip of the year, you can imagine my relief to have him safely back and my joy at hearing reports of progress toward establishing a rapport with the Afghan farmers.

The farmers' initial reluctance was understandable. Back then, US government representatives charged with reviving Afghanistan's economy wanted the fastest possible route to success. They'd quickly initiate agricultural programs, then pull out. Roots of Peace preferred sustainable, long-term solutions that included identifying new, higher-yield, and higher-value crops such as fruits and nuts, then spent months training farmers in modern agricultural techniques.

It turned out that Afghanistan's climate was similar to that of California's Central Valley. Fruits and nuts, huge industries in California, could be lucrative in Afghanistan as well, but it would take time to help farmers acclimate to these new crops. Afghanistan's main resource, arable land, had the potential to produce excellent fruits and nuts. There aren't too many places in the world that can do so, and they had the right climate to make those items a great natural resource. Unfortunately, there were also so many obstacles ahead for them.

Each time Gary returned home, he would share stories of establishing our foundation in Afghanistan. I yearned to go, but he told me that it was too dangerous for a woman to be negotiating with various tribes in a male-dominated society—especially at the beginning, when trust was needed.

Working with political and military officials in the removal of landmines, there have been countless times I have walked into a room and been the only woman. I felt a familiar sting of bias as some donors voiced skepticism over the odds of success in updating ancient farming practices in such a remote part of the world and sarcastically called us "the California fruits, nuts, and flakes team." Sharing my vision to eradicate landmines and plant grapevines is a solid business model that demonstrated measurable ripple effects around the world. Yet, many times, the greatest challenge is still to be taken seriously. To counter this challenge, I remind myself of a famous Theodore Roosevelt quote: "It is not the critic who counts, nor the man who points out how the strong man stumbles, or where the doer of deeds could have done them better. The credit belongs to the man who is actually in the arena . . ."

By 2003, our professional staff had also begun to expand. We partnered with experts from UC Davis for technical expertise and with veterans of agricultural-export marketing from Agland Investment Services, the firm that had pioneered growing orchids and delivering them to America's supermarkets. With their guidance, we expanded our initial focus on grapes to pomegranates in Kandahar, apples in Ghazni, almonds in Wardak, cherries in Badakhshan, oranges in Jalalabad, and saffron in Herat. Roots of Peace spread across the country, which was once dubbed "the garden of Central Asia."

Later that year, Gary announced he would again be returning to Afghanistan, and this time he planned to take our son Tucker with him as a rite of passage after Tucker's high school graduation. It was bad enough having my husband in a dangerous war zone, but worse to think of my eighteen-year-old son there. I begged Gary not to take him, but he and Tucker held fast to their intention to travel together. In a tender gesture, they took me outside to see the full moon.

"Mom," said Tucker, "I know you love me and are just trying to protect me, but I'm a man now. Can't you just trust our decision?"

I was so touched by that phrase "I'm a man now" that I melted.

Gary added, "Both of us completely support your vision, Heidi. You need to trust us to take this important initiative to the next level."

Letting my son go to such an obviously dangerous place was one of the hardest decisions of my life.

The next day, Gary said to me, "We're not going to pretend we're heroes. We're going because we believe in Roots of Peace, and we can't do the work from here. We need to stand in the fields and see for ourselves what crops can be planted, what equipment will be needed. There's no other way to do this."

Essentially, he called my bluff. Still, it was excruciating to drive them to San Francisco International Airport for their flight to Kabul. At the airport, they met other members of this exploratory mission. It all felt strange: We weren't a military family, but my nearest and dearest were, once again, intentionally flying into a war zone.

They arrived safely in Afghanistan and were soon in the barren vineyards of the Shomali Plain to make their assessments. Shortly after their arrival, a storm broke, sending large hailstones raining down on the minefields. The weight of just one large hailstone was enough to trigger a landmine, and they were in the middle of a vast minefield. Their path was outlined by painted rocks, and their pretour briefing had stressed that, for obvious reasons, they could not run in the minefield. But as the hail intensified, dozens of deminers, along with Gary and Tucker, dashed to safety in the fastest walk you have ever seen, using their heavy plastic face shields to cover their heads while the hail pelted their shoulders. Dangers from so many directions.

Meanwhile, back home, I worried constantly about my husband's and son's well-being. One night, my heart started to palpitate, and I was rushed to the hospital. The doctors prescribed anxiety drugs, but that was not what I needed. I was in a spiritual crisis, feeling alone, isolated, and extremely guilty over placing my family at mortal risk. I called Father Kevin Longworth in Ireland, and together we prayed for hours. He assured me that I had made the right decision and needed to trust my husband and son. His words sustained me through the many long weeks to come.

A short time later, I flew to Washington, DC, with Lynn Davison, a Marin County mother of two small boys whose brother worked at the State Department, and we were introduced to Nitin Madhav of the US Agency for International Development (USAID). During the meeting, I also met Doug Tinsler and Ron Ivey of Chemonics International, a for-profit development company working around the globe with decades of experience operating in complex social and political environments. My hope was that Chemonics would agree to accept Roots of Peace as a sub-contractor in Afghanistan. I introduced Roots of Peace by saying, "Our vision is to turn mines to vines in Afghanistan." Tinsler shook his head, as if he hadn't quite heard correctly, and he called several of his staff into the room and asked me to repeat myself.

"Our dream is to turn mines to vines in Afghanistan," I said. Then I explained the "economics of peace" that was the foundation of our work: Raise funds to hire demining companies to clear fields of mines, then train farmers to implement modern farming techniques.

"Fresh grapes and raisins were once a staple of Afghan farmers," I explained. "Then the drug trade took over. If the land can be reclaimed through landmine removal, alternatives crops to poppies and opium can be substituted. Our expertise includes helping local farmers decide whether to plant grapes or other produce for sale to international markets."

The presentation was well received, and Bob Flick and Frank Kenefick of Chemonics agreed to fly out to San Rafael to meet with Gary and discuss a business approach to the mission in Afghanistan.

Once again, the meeting was conducted at Roots of Peace world head-quarters—our home. After Gary's successful career in the world of high tech, agribusiness had absorbed his attention and brought out a side of him I had not seen before. He was genuinely excited about rebuilding a new market in Afghanistan and saw the potential for the deserving farmers. Working side by side with me in our basement wasn't nearly as glamorous as the offices where he had worked previously, but he jumped right in, eager to help.

Gary reached out to Agland Investment Services, based in Marin County, to educate himself on global agribusiness. He met regularly with Bill Mott and Bill Scott, who ran the global management and consulting firm, which focuses on food security, agriculture, and natural resource management. For decades, their team has served as a trusted adviser to governments and corporate entities to enhance work in the agricultural sector. Agland was a wonderful partner and mentor. Gary already pos-sessed valuable expertise in business development and could easily have found another job in the tech industry, but that kind of work didn't excite him nearly as much as the prospect of improving the economy of an entire country.

The next day, Gary met with the directors of Chemonics, the lead-ing contractor for the Rebuilding Afghan Markets Program (RAMP). Roots of Peace had been chosen to serve as the implementing part-ner for Chemonics, which operates in more than 150 countries and enjoys a reputation for finding creative ways to restore order to com-munities suffering from the misfortunes of war. Unfortunately, their staff in Afghanistan had gone through numerous changes, and each new director had had a different idea for moving the nation forward economically.

After six months of discussion, our consortium of Agland, Chemonics, Roots of Peace, and UC Davis was awarded a $6 million contract from USAID to rescue Afghanistan's grape industry. For Roots of Peace, this was a new beginning. Two and half years of funding would allow us to formalize our team and our efforts. Bill Mott and Bill Scott at Agland, Bob Flick, Frank Kenefick, and Ron Ivey at Chemonics, and Pat Brown and Jim Hill at UC Davis had helped get us to this award. Without any one of them, our path would have been drastically different. Now we had to implement.

The farmland in the Shomali Plain was barely usable. Farmers were growing grapes on mounds with the grapes clustered close to the ground, where disease and molds infected them and where the land itself was seeded with landmines. We could tell that the grapes showed great promise, but there would be many steps before we could take them to better markets. Furthermore, there was no cold chain in Afghanistan for exports. Harvested grapes require cold storage and early-hour harvesting to ensure the highest quality, but the farmers were unfamiliar with such modern harvesting techniques and had no money to implement them.

Roots of Peace, in partnership with Agland and UC Davis, started by first identifying a demonstration plot where we could show farmers how grapes were successfully cultivated in California's Central Valley—for example, by building trellises to raise the vines off the ground and by properly pruning the vines. To transition the vines from bush grown to trellising, we had to prune back around twelve canes, leaving only two that we would train up onto the trellis, eventually cutting one of the remaining canes to leave only one.

The farmers had never seen anyone cut the vines so severely. They could not understand how cutting off most of the vine would increase yields, and they all refused to participate in the pilot. We had thirty-three Afghan agriculture extension agents at that time, and Gary told each of them that they had to find at least one farmer to convert two rows of their vineyard, or he might terminate their positions. Trellising was critical to the program, and we had to start this pilot.

All the extension agents found one vineyard to participate. Mostly they belonged to relatives of the agents, who participated as a favor to help a relative keep a job. Gary assured them that the vines would grow back stronger and with heartier yields.

As I watched all this unfold from afar, I continued to pray for his safety and was comforted by the Bible verse (John 15:1–8) "I am the true vine, and my Father is the vinedresser. Every branch in me that does not bear fruit, he takes away; and every branch that bears fruit, he prunes so that it may bear more fruit. I am the vine, you are the branches."

Within four months, the farmers and the Roots of Peace agriculture extension team saw the results and were convinced: The numerous tiny clusters of grapes were spread all over the vines. Farmers asked to have their entire vineyards trellised. A year later, we documented the yield increase at 107 percent. Our first success was very visible and substantial. Farmers did not doubt us after that; they followed whatever we advised, as we had finally earned their trust.

In addition to the planting program, our experts installed a small cold-storage and packhouse facility in the Mir Bacha Kot District of Kabul Province and implemented modern packing techniques at food-processing centers. The team trained Afghan traders on food safety, sorting, and grading and introduced corrugated boxes and branding of

Afghan grapes. They showed the traders how to sort and pack cluster grapes for export, replacing the burlap sacks that farmers had previously been using to drag their fruit to market. Within three years, farmers across Afghanistan were earning two to three times more from growing and selling their high-value crops than they had previously from growing and selling opium, and Afghan traders were realizing revenues they had not enjoyed since before the Soviet invasion.

When Roots of Peace returned in the spring, many of the wooden trellis posts had been cut down. Puzzled, we asked the Afghan elders why. Their reply was very matter-of-fact: That winter had been the coldest on record, and the wooden posts had been needed to build fires to cook and stay warm. The response taught us not to make assumptions when working in cultures other than our own and to take time to better educate ourselves concerning local conditions. That year, we adjusted our techniques and introduced cement trellis posts after Gary designed the posts with the help of my father, Robert Thomas, who owned McNear Block Company and had experience in cement construction. We convinced four Afghan businesses to begin manufacturing, selling, and distributing these trellis posts throughout the country, and with our tutelage, they refined their manufacturing and went on to make millions of these posts.

With the $6 million in funding, we were able to finally catapult Roots of Peace out of the basement of our Kühn family home and rent office space on Fourth Street in downtown San Rafael. The move up also marked the first time we were able to pay ourselves a modest salary and purchase health insurance for our family. After nearly ten years of gearing up, it felt like we were finally on our way.

Over the next dozen years, Gary made more than fifty trips to Afghanistan. The next step was helping Afghan farmers build relations with importers in India, Pakistan, the United Arab Emirates, Russia, and Canada. Securing partnerships with international customers meant farmers were no longer forced to sell to local markets at unfair prices.

The US military and NATO forces began recognizing Roots of Peace as an effective example of how to help an emerging nation lift itself to healthier economic levels. Every week, we held conference calls with the US Army's Agribusiness Development Teams (ADTs) as they reported on the progress of planting fruit trees in remote provinces and sought our advice.

It was quite an experience, participating as a civilian on calls over secured military phone lines that might begin with, "Ma'am, this is Colonel Howard Shauer, reporting from Kandahar." Each province called in with its report, one at a time, and each call reminded me that these were the voices of men and women working on the front lines to improve the lives of Afghan farmers and their families with techniques developed by Roots of Peace. Those calls made the war in Afghanistan quite personal, something more than an article in a newspaper. They were evidence that military forces and market forces working together could help turn swords into plowshares by replacing guns with shovels.

The reports from American soldiers risking their lives in Afghanistan reminded me of a quote from Jeremiah: "I will restore you to health and heal your wounds."[5]

---

5. Jeremiah 30:17.

CHAPTER SIX

PLANTING PEACE

Tell me and I'll forget.
Show me, and I may not remember.
Involve me, and I'll understand.

—UNKNOWN

In the six years since I had started Roots of Peace in the basement of our home, our team had made tangible progress in Croatia and was now starting in Afghanistan, clearing landmines and introducing techniques and equipment needed to plant and harvest high-yield crops. Our work was conducted in countries suffering from the consequences of deadly fighting and dire poverty, and even with the best of intentions, our little group could hope to make only a modest contribution toward restoring a degree of normalcy. Still, despite our limitations, miracles had taken place before our eyes. Substantial funding had arrived from unexpected sources. Support and encouragement had come from highly placed leaders in government and industry. Despite our lack of formal training in the peace process, we had seen the difference a hand of friendship could make in the lives of tens of thousands of local farmers and their families. As it is said, great journeys begin with a small step.

If ever there was an example of what small steps could accomplish, it came in the form of pennies in the summer of 2003.

Earlier that year, local journalist Cheryl Jennings had called me to discuss doing an interview about Roots of Peace for ABC7 News. I brought my sixteen-year-old daughter, Kyleigh, to television station KGO in San Francisco, and over lunch we learned that Cheryl had firsthand experience with landmines in Kosovo. The three of us discussed what we might do together. Why not create a program run by children, she suggested, a program that would benefit children who were victims of war? Inspired by President George W. Bush's America's Fund for Afghan Children initiative, which invited every American child to contribute $1 to the relief fund, and Oprah's Angel Network, Kyleigh expressed a desire to make a similar campaign her summer project. The goal would be to collect millions of pennies and use the money to fund removal of landmines and rebuild schools and soccer fields.

"Change! One penny at a time!" became her battle cry.

On September 11, 2003, Kyleigh launched the Roots of Peace Children's Penny Campaign at Del Mar Middle School in Tiburon, and dozens of teenagers joined in the summer project. My San Rafael High School friends from the 1970s, Denise Bernstein Abbett and Nonie Greene, had children who attended Del Mar, which was also Gary's alma mater. Gary's sister, Leslie Doyle, had two children, Conor and Laurel, who also attended schools in Tiburon's Reed Union School District. Their father, Al Kühn, had been mayor of Tiburon, and together we had many local friends and supporters. Lynn Davison, a Marin mother of two boys, assisted with logistics, along with

Allison Bainbridge and Sue DeVinney. The peace movement of the 1970s was back!

The energized group of Kyleigh's school friends reached out and persuaded Mary Jane Burke, Marin County's superintendent of schools, and more than seventy schools to take part. Don Leisey, the former superintendent of San Rafael City Schools, donated printed canisters to gather the pennies at local stores throughout the San Francisco Bay Area. Thanks to reports by journalists like the *Marin Independent Journal*'s Beth Ashley, word of the program spread. Within a matter of weeks, Kyleigh was receiving letters daily from children around the country, including some in New York and New Jersey who had lost their parents in the 9/11 tragedy. Along with hundreds of letters came tens of thousands of pennies in cardboard boxes and glass jars, cloth sacks and metal containers. By the fall of 2005, Kyleigh and her fellow activists had collected $50,000 in pennies to fund various projects.

The day came to deliver the mountain of pennies to the bank. To attract press coverage of the occasion, the students convinced local firefighters to drive their hook-and-ladder trucks to the school's playground. Police, sharing the spirit of the initiative, arrived in a half-dozen squad cars. Joan Capurro, manager of the Bank of Marin, enlisted the bank's Loomis, Fargo & Co. armored vehicles. The gathering at Kyleigh's school featured the true stars of the campaign: the students who had worked tirelessly for months to collect so many pennies. Cheryl Jennings hosted the proceedings, which featured keynote speeches by local celebrities such as youth counselor and comedian Michael Pritchard. The school chorus sang John Lennon's iconic hymn to world peace, "Imagine," with customized lyrics:

Imagine there's no landmines, it isn't hard to do,
No hell beneath you, above us only blue.
Imagine all the people, living life in peace . . .
You may say that I'm a dreamer, but I'm not the only one.

Big, strong firefighters and police officers grew misty-eyed when the students saluted the American flag and sang "America the Beautiful." Then the armored van drivers loaded the mountain of pennies into their vehicles and drove them to Bank of Marin. The hard work had paid off, and the $50,000 in coins eventually helped build new schools on former minefields in the villages of Mir Bacha Kot and Bam Saray in Afghanistan.

"Change! One penny at a time!"

As Roots of Peace's reputation for getting the job done expanded, so did the number of our partnerships, and soon we had signed agreements with the US Department of Defense to plant thousands of pine trees along the city streets of Kabul, extending as far as Hamid Karzai International Airport. Arriving visitors were then greeted with a vision of nature restored to a place where war had stripped it away.

In early 2005, Gary and I arrived at the headquarters of the US Department of Agriculture to meet with Patricia Sheikh, deputy administrator of the USDA's Foreign Agricultural Service, to describe our efforts in Afghanistan. Sheikh, intrigued, brought in members of her senior staff to join our conversation, including Liliana Bachelder and Roger Mireles. Based on the Roots of Peace track record, they agreed to represent our cause to FAS and USDA decision-makers and recommend us as a partner project.

A USDA wheat-monetization program was approved and signed in 2008, granting Roots of Peace the right to receive 12,500 tons of wheat that could be sold in-country for a total market value of $3,273,176. The three-year program allowed proceeds from the sale to be used to expand production of grapes, improve postharvest services, and advance business development. Based on field surveys and in consultation with USDA officials, Roots of Peace selected twenty-five districts in three provinces, Ghazni, Logar and Wardak, to implement these objectives. These were particularly war-torn regions, too dangerous for many other organizations, but Roots of Peace had earned the trust of local Afghans, who saw firsthand the results of our nonprofit work.

The journey of the wheat was long and complex. Trucks transported the heavy sacks of wheat grown in the American Midwest to the shores of Virginia, where cargo ships set out to bring the bounty across the Atlantic to Pakistan. From there, the large burlap sacks were relayed by trucks through the Khyber Pass to be sold at market in Kabul. Gary and I traveled to Afghanistan to personally greet the shipment. When we arrived, we saw lines of trucks filled with sacks of flour boldly stamped "USA." Together, we jumped into the back of a truck. Then Mohammad Sharif Osmani, the Roots of Peace country director for Afghanistan, who had been our translator during our first visit to the country, began the long process of selling the wheat flour to Afghan traders.

Over the years, our reputation for going the extra mile earned us additional contracts with the Asian Development Bank, the European Union, and the World Bank. During these years of rapid growth, one of our proudest moments came when US Army general John F. Campbell presented us with a traditionally folded American flag and made us honorary members of the 101st Airborne Division's 506th Infantry

Regiment, honoring Roots of Peace's work in harmonizing military forces and market forces in pursuit of peace in Afghanistan.

Our organization had achieved a level of support and recognition we could never have imagined back in the days of stuffing envelopes and balancing babies in the basement of our home. Small steps were propelling us toward a very bright future.

CHAPTER SEVEN

IN PRINCESS DIANA'S FOOTSTEPS

The Earth is but one country and mankind its citizens.

—BAHA'I PROVERB

For twenty-seven years, between 1975 and 2002, a bitter and deadly conflict was fought in Angola in the aftermath of its independence from Portugal. This had been a proxy war between the Soviet Union and the United States, ostensibly fought over the competing ideals of Marxist-Leninist ideology and capitalism, but as always, it was the defenseless who really suffered. More than a half-million Angolans died in those years, and another million were displaced from their homes or exiled.

According to the *Landmine Monitor* report, Angola had become the third most landmine-infested country in the world, after Afghanistan and Cambodia. Contrary to popular belief, Angola is an agriculturally rich country, so much so that, properly administered, the nation could feed much of sub-Saharan Africa. But the presence of an estimated ten million landmines was preventing cultivation of crops. Shortly after the main conflict ended in 2002, Roots of Peace began its campaign to restore functioning agriculture in Angola. I had expressed my passion for following in the footsteps of the late Princess Diana, and yearned to clear the landmines in the same province of Huambo in Angola where she walked in January 1997. I could not believe that the world was so blind as to leave these landmines buried in the ground over five years after she had raised global landmine awareness. Angola has fertile soils spanning more than fifty-seven million hectares of agricultural land, yet it remained the most heavily mined country on the continent of Africa. If the landmines were removed, Angola could feed millions of people. Something had to be done.

Something began to be done when the State Department's PM/WRA agency, which appreciated and respected the inroads Roots of Peace had made elsewhere in the world, provided $200,000 to jump-start the effort so we could establish an office in Luanda, the capital of Angola.

When Gary and I arrived, we heard chilling tales from landmine survivors who were too poor to feed themselves and their families because they lived on land riddled with mines. The manner in which the landmines had been planted was diabolically ingenious. Protracted war had worsened an already impoverished place by denying farmers access to their own land, and most of the mines lay buried along the roads and in the farmland surrounding the towns and villages where renewal was just beginning. In effect, the farmers were surrounded, held hostage by landmines.

One tale that embodies the nation's tragic condition involved an Angolan woman, Ana Paula. Her older sister, Theresa, told me her story. When Ana Paula was eight months pregnant, food was scarce and she feared for the health of her soon-to-be-born child. Near her home was a small grove of ripe mango trees, but Ana Paula knew the rumors: Landmines had been planted throughout the grove.

"Still, my sister decided to walk through the grove," Theresa told me through her tears. "She made it to the mango trees. Then, as she was picking a mango, a landmine exploded beneath her feet."

Tears flowed down Theresa's cheeks. "I had to watch my sister give birth while having a leg amputated at the same time."

A similar story had been told to me by Ambassador Donald Steinberg at our initial fundraiser at the Robert Mondavi Winery in Napa Valley in 1999, but hearing these stories firsthand in a landmine-affected country was riveting.

The Children's Penny Campaign also contributed funds to remove landmines in Huambo, Angola's third-largest city. This was one of the places visited by Princess Diana when she was the world's most recognizable spokesperson for demining. As we arrived in Huambo, Gary and I were shocked to learn how many landmines were still in the ground. While the media had made much of Diana's death in August 1997, little had been done to realize her life's mission.

Working with the HALO Trust, Roots of Peace raised awareness for the removal of landmines in an area that had once been a children's soccer field. Hollywood actress Diane Baker dubbed her voice on a Roots of Peace video edited at San Francisco's Academy of Art University. After rebuilding the field and making it again available to aspiring soccer champions, we spent the balance of the year raising the necessary funds to buy children's crutches and prosthetic limbs through our partnership with Catholic Relief Services. The Children's Penny Campaign contributed $10,000 to build the soccer field on the former minefield. Our moment of greatest satisfaction came when we were at last able to watch young Angolans play soccer on land that, a short time before, had been a death trap.

Our next step was to evaluate the indigenous animals injured by landmines. Roots of Peace partnered with Conservation International to clear mines and restore ancient elephant migration routes linking Botswana with Zambia and Angola to form a transfrontier conservation area. It is estimated that 120,000 elephants, whose numbers are growing at 5 percent annually, would be able to move north into Angola and Zambia if the mines were cleared. As we traveled through the country, we saw many carcasses of elephants, majestic creatures killed by landmines either instantly or slowly, as they bled to death from lost limbs. For centuries, these large animals had lived in alignment with humans as they migrated along the Chobe River in the heart of Africa. But once soldiers seeded these ancient migration routes with landmines, elephants accidentally triggered them and either died or lost a leg or a trunk. Without their limbs and the ability to migrate, the wounded elephants quickly depleted nearby food sources and were forced to eat the villages' trees. Angry villagers ended up turning on the elephants with guns, so the threat to the elephants was twofold.

Soon after our arrival, I climbed into a helicopter with wildlife conservationist Olivier Langrand and elephant ecologist Mike Chase on a Conservation International mission to place GPS tracking devices on elephants. Mike, born in Botswana, had worked to preserve the Okavango

Delta by applying creative ideas and progressive research to help elephants, and he knew many of them by name.

Flying over the African wilderness, seeing the migration of giraffes, and searching for elephants in their natural setting was an extraordinary experience. Once a herd was located, the conservationists used non-lethal dart guns to temporarily anesthetize the elephants, then landed and placed GPS collars around their necks. From then on, the scientists were able to track the herds' migrations and take preventative measures when they strayed too close to landmines.

Because one huge bull elephant named Duke already had a tracking collar we were going to retrieve, we could signal the ground team where to go from the helicopter. Once the team darted him, we followed him until he dropped. But Duke was strong, leading us on an international chase over the border from Namibia into Zimbabwe. The ground crew ran through the Kalahari sands, and when we finally caught up with Duke, he was resting on his chest, struggling to breathe because all his weight was pressing down on his lungs. It was not until the entire team from Conservation International and Roots of Peace pressed our shoulders into Duke that we were able to push the huge animal over, and Duke was good after that. His herd hovered close by, watching us perform our measurements and replace his collar with a new tracking device. Once the sedative wore off, Duke jumped up, a little dazed, then sauntered toward his herd to help lead the way so that researchers could identify the alternative migration routes elephants had developed in response to the man-made tragedy of landmines.

Next, Gary and I flew to Cuando Cubango, a heavily mined region of Angola. As our airplane landed, the pilot said, "There are hundreds of live landmines visibly sticking up from both sides of the runway. Just one mistake, and we will detonate a landmine. We must be precise in our landing." Gary and I looked out the window and saw the landmines clearly protruding from the ground, visible to the naked eye. This area had been the site of the second-largest tank battle in the continent's history, and the battlefield looked pretty much the same as it had when the battle had ended: You could still see the tracks the tanks made as they advanced until they met their demise. It was like a military-strategy case study unfolding before us.

We arrived for our meetings with the government to discuss the landmines issue, only to learn they had been canceled. The two top government leaders scheduled to attend had been driving to the meeting when they swerved to avoid a wild animal that had darted onto the road. Their car triggered an antitank mine, the passengers were instantly killed, and the Angolan ministry was in mourning. If their own government officials were not safe from mines, who was?

Later, we learned about the Angolans' twofold system to reduce the mine threat on public roads. First, a large metal detector was used to sweep a road and locate metal-cased antitank mines. Second, a heavy detonation trailer, designed to detonate any active mines, passed down the road. Deminers knew they would not find all the mines, and to warn civilian drivers, they used red flags, painted sticks, and plastic tape to mark uncleared areas.

Driving through Angola, we saw dozens of children carrying brightly colored plastic chairs on their heads as they walked to and from school. Education was the surest way to lift these children from poverty, but roads to classes were lined with danger.

On the morning of July 7, 2005, Gary and I returned to Huambo to assess the results of the demining efforts and other Roots of Peace programs. Two years earlier, we had been appalled that the fields were still mined so long after Princess Diana's death, and our response had been to expand our outreach from Afghanistan to Angola with the Children's Penny Campaign under Kyleigh's directorship.

With millions of pennies, we were able to build a soccer field, and the local children were once again able to play on the land surrounding their homes. The renovated sports area in Huambo had been renamed after Princess Diana.

One of the Angolan boys recognized us and joked, "Now we play on three legs instead of two—one good leg and two crutches!" Then he laughed freely.

What an astonishing thing to be able to laugh at one's own misfortunes like that.

As time went by, it became more and more upsetting to me that the rest of the world was consumed by other headlines and other causes, however worthy, and paid so little attention to what seemed to me to be one of the most pressing issues of our time. How could people not understand the urgency of removing landmines where innocent children played?

Gary and I talked about the world's short attention span. "I know people have their own concerns," I said, "but how can anyone decline getting involved in something so clear and urgent as saving children from landmines? The danger is imminent. It's happening *as we speak*."

I remember ABC7 News anchor Cheryl Jennings reminding me that "many people in the world just can't relate to the concern about landmines. After all, landmines don't affect ordinary Americans—unless they are in the military. So, it's not a daily concern. I get that." Still, she was adamant, as was I, that what could happen, if and when people did start to care about the destructive power of landmines and take action, would be nothing less than a miracle. Cheryl believed in the efforts of Roots of Peace so strongly that she convinced her news station to send a crew to cover our story in three countries. Through her news lens, she was able to share stories of empathy and compassion and raise awareness.

"You see it up close, so you feel it the strongest," Gary said, trying to make me feel better. "What this whole new career has reminded me is what a privilege it is to live in California and coach healthy young boys who will never suffer such atrocities. I'll never take it for granted."

The hot summer sun continued to rise on that July morning as we continued our inspection of the HALO Trust's progress in Huambo. Gary and I suited up in flak jackets and helmets with protective glass shields, the same standard protection Princess Diana had worn when she was there. It was extremely hot inside the heavy gear, but as we walked through the live minefields, careful to never step away from the demined narrow path, we were very pleased by what we saw: HALO technicians had trained the locals well in proper and safe landmine-removal techniques.

An hour or so into our visit, we heard screams. Looking up, we saw a dark cloud approaching us. The Angolan deminers shouted at us to stand absolutely still—no movement. I could see fright in the eyes of the team that had brought us there. I whispered to our guide, "What's wrong? Please tell me what the danger is."

"Mrs. Kühn," he said, "please do not panic, but you must know that this is quite serious. Lives may be lost. Whatever happens, do not take off your face mask."

I swallowed hard. What was the danger? What was that black cloud descending on us? I stood very, very still. Then a tornado of killer bees—tens of thousands of them—swarmed over the minefield and flew directly toward us, and the noise was overwhelming as the tidal wave of bees slammed up against the visor on my protective helmet and then flew on. All I could think of was my youngest son, Christian, who was now eight years old and anticipating the safe arrival of his parents back home for his summer vacation.

My arms and legs were exposed, and my instinctive reaction was to run away as fast as I could. But I had been instructed otherwise, and it was clear that if I lost my cool now, I'd be inviting the thick cloud of killer bees to focus on me. Gary and I somehow managed to stay still, holding hands, while the deafening sound of bees beat down on us, their lethal, bulletlike bodies hitting us as we stood immobile. The deafening buzz of the bees was the worst, bone chilling, my worst nightmare come true. There was black everywhere, as if we stood in the eye of a storm, the *thunk-thunk* sound of bees hitting my helmet one after another—*thunk, thunk, thunk*. Every fiber in my body wanted me to flee as adrenaline coursed through me. I could no longer look at the bees crashing into my face mask, so I closed my eyes and prayed.

Then there was silence.

We looked around, gasping for breath, assessing the situation. We were all alive. I had maybe a half-dozen stings on my arms and legs. Slowly, we took off our gear, turned, and walked back into the safety of the HALO Trust compound—only to confront yet another lethal threat, though this time from afar. CNN was announcing that a series of coordinated suicide bombers had attacked central London, targeting civilians using public transportation during the morning rush hour. Three bombs, detonated in quick succession, had killed 52 people and injured more than 700. Many of the Angolan deminers had families in the United Kingdom and were on the phone at once, terrified that they had lost family members.

Swarms of bees and swarms of terrorists collided on that terrifying day, July 7, 2005.

Later that week, I had the honor of meeting the first lady of Angola, Ana Paula Dos Santos, who presented me with a prized personal possession from her home: an ebony sculpture of a proud African woman, offered as a tribute, she said, to my courage. I told her that women who lived surrounded by minefields each day were far more courageous than I would ever be. I invited the first lady to visit the United States and go with me to the Isaiah Wall, a staircase backdrop located across the street from the United Nations named after the source of the biblical inscription engraved on it, and she agreed. Together, we would plant the Angolan national flower at the Roots of Peace Garden beneath this wall of inspiration.

That week, I had the honor of introducing Dos Santos to the Clinton Foundation's Clinton Global Initiative. Along with Dos Santos, the event was attended by representatives from the State Department and Maurice Tempelsman, a Belgian-American businessman and diamond merchant and longtime companion of Jacqueline Kennedy Onassis, former first lady of the United States. It was all quite heady stuff for me, never having been a part of such circles of power and influence, and the week reinforced a growing awareness in my heart that, as my dear Granny McNear used to say, "For unto whomsoever much is given, of him shall be much required."[6]

---

6. Luke 12:48.

I've always really wanted my children to learn that we need to walk the Earth with humility, grace, and respect for all we have been given. I've taught them that wealth does not come from what glitters around you; it can be sourced only from within. The currency of the heart has by far been the most priceless gift that has planted the roots of peace on many continents.

Our mission to plant the roots of peace on Earth was now being fulfilled in Africa, the third continent in our anti-landmine activism, another piece of this sacred global puzzle we are creating. Each small step was bringing us closer to our goal of helping eradicate landmines from the Earth. As part of the proceedings, we planted the Angolan national flower, the Welwitschia, on the grounds of the Roots of Peace Garden at the Isaiah Wall. Our youngest son, Christian, age eight, carried the large ceremonial shovel as a representative of future generations of humble peacemakers.

CHAPTER EIGHT

THE SILK ROAD

I never see what has been done.
I only see what remains to be done.

—UNKNOWN

Since our work had begun in 2001, Roots of Peace had dramatically expanded the size of its teams and had trained hundreds of thousands of farmers and their families in all thirty-four provinces of Afghanistan. With funds generously provided by Diane Disney Miller, we were able to remove more than 100,000 landmines and other UXOs with UNMAS and the HALO Trust in the Shomali Plain, located north of Kabul. Those former minefields were now producing almonds, apples, apricots, cherries, grapes, and pomegranates, bearing evidence that mines to vines was indeed a viable formula.

Our next visit to Afghanistan was in August 2005, which happened to coincide with our daughter Kyleigh's entrance into UC Santa Barbara.

As we had done for our son Brooks, Gary and I extended to Kyleigh an invitation to join us in Afghanistan, and she accepted. ABC7 News anchor Cheryl Jennings joined us to film a five-part series on the work of Roots of Peace.

It was an intrepid journey as we three women boarded the aircraft from Dubai to Kabul with black scarfs tied over our heads. This was my first journey to Afghanistan, and Mike Clark was our cameraman, doubling as our bodyguard. As the aircraft flew over the Hindu Kush mountain range, where peaks reach to the sky as high as 25,000 feet, I felt an enormous surge of pride in aiding the innocent Afghan families we had promised to help after the tragedy of the 9/11 attacks. Looking down on the panoramic landscape, I wondered how people could ever justify planting landmines on the one Earth we were given to steward.

We arrived in Afghanistan and drove to Mir Bacha Kot, the village where, the year before, Roots of Peace had helped modernize grape farming and installed a cold-storage facility. Technically, the war had ended, but it was still very dangerous for foreigners, especially women, to travel through countryside that had been the Taliban's front line during the war. We put on flak jackets, and I tucked a set of rosary beads inside my vest.

When we arrived at Mir Bacha Kot, farmers greeted us warmly and expressed heartfelt appreciation for how much Roots of Peace had improved their lives. They explained that thanks to our efforts, their vineyards were producing a rich harvest, and in particular they were grateful that their children would no longer have to depend on outside relief services for the basic necessities of life.

In an act of gratitude, the farmers pulled prayer beads from their pockets and began reciting verses from the Holy Qur'an, and I instinctively pulled out my rosary beads and joined them in prayer. To my astonishment, the farmers joined hands, reached out to hold my hands, and recited verses that, I later learned, expressed the idea that we serve the same God and are all daughters and sons of Abraham. I would not have expected religious Muslim men to hold hands with a non-Muslim woman. Yet somehow, standing there on the edge of a minefield that together we had transformed into a vineyard, the gesture seemed altogether fitting. They later explained that Mary was the most respected woman in the Holy Qur'an, and they were grateful that a mother had come to bring compassion to their children.

Toward the end of our visit, while inspecting the cold-storage facility funded by USAID, Kyleigh noticed a group of children sitting on the ground beneath a giant grapevine. She asked one of our Roots of Peace Afghan drivers, Torelei, why they were outdoors on such a hot day. He looked embarrassed and cast his eyes toward the ground. His own children were among them, he said, and he quietly explained that the children had no school building. There was no place for them to be other than sitting outdoors on the dirt in the blazing sun. Kyleigh approached the children and was astonished to see that they shared only one chalkboard among them and were using rocks as writing implements. They spoke no English and had never seen a blond, blue-eyed person like Kyleigh before. Despite the lack of a common language, they made shapes of imaginary masks with their fingers and communicated by singing songs and laughing.

Sometimes life provides moments that become a calling, and this proved to be one such moment for Kyleigh. As we packed up to leave, she looked at me and Cheryl and said, "I want to build a school for these children on the former minefield across the road." All the hard work in raising pennies for peace had paid off, and she had located the perfect site to benefit the Afghan children. Something in her certainty over the need to build a school had me catching my breath with pride.

For six years, I had lived with the troubling fear that my commitment to Roots of Peace came at the cost of my responsibility as a mother. My children were entitled to their mother's love and attention. I constantly worried that I had compromised their emotional well-being under the pretext of wanting to help the larger world. It is a worry that has never completely gone away, but in that moment, hearing Kyleigh boldly declare her own intentions to do something for children who were not family or fellow Americans, children whose language she did not speak, whose culture and religion were alien to her own, children who deserved her compassion for the simple reason that they were humans like us—in that moment, she did more to appease my doubting heart than any acknowledgment from governments or corporations could ever do. Aspiring do-gooders like me need such moments to reassure us that in seeking to increase humanity for others, we haven't lost our own.

Our trio of women next visited the International Committee of the Red Cross (ICRC) clinic in Kabul, where more than a hundred landmine survivors arrived each day, hoping for treatment and an artificial limb. We met with the resident physician, Dr. Alberto Cairo, who had worked tirelessly for decades to serve landmine victims of the region. Cheryl Jennings conducted an on-camera interview, after which we wandered through the clinic, capturing B-roll footage, while Kyleigh spoke with some of the teenage survivors.

Kyleigh approached a young man who had lost a leg from the hip down. He introduced himself as Fawad Afa and, coincidentally, it turned out they had been born on the same day: May 1, 1987. At age ten, Fawad had run onto a minefield to retrieve a soccer ball that had been kicked out of bounds by his team. His mother had warned him of the danger lurking outside the soccer field area, but the ball was the only one in Fawad's village, and he was the team leader.

Boom!

Fawad's leg was blown off, and he lay dying, but neighbors managed to rescue him.

Cheryl and her crew entered the room. Hearing Fawad's story, they photographed Kyleigh and her new friend. Then they began packing up their gear.

"Mom," Kyleigh said, "you can't just take a photo and walk away. You have to give him a job."

"What does he want to do?" I asked, knowing in my heart that she was right. "Before he lost his leg, did he have any dreams for the future?"

Fawad heard me and knew enough English to answer for himself. "I love to play soccer," he said.

That's how Fawad Afa got hired as soccer coach for the official Roots of Peace girls' soccer team in Afghanistan, his first paid employment, and our first teenage Afghan employee.

Once Fawad was outfitted with crutches, he showed up every day to coach the soccer team, and he proved himself to be an insightful and capable team leader who eventually led them to national prominence. Its fame even earned the girls an invitation to meet US Secretary of State Condoleezza Rice at the US Consulate in Kabul, where Rice congratulated them on their success.

In 2007, Roots of Peace sent the entire soccer team to compete in San Patrignano, Italy, led once again by their gifted coach. CNN producer Flavia Taggiasco helped me coordinate the trip for a dozen beautiful Afghan teenage girls, and we suddenly recognized our responsibility to protect them from admiring Italian boys. Swimming in the salt water of the Adriatic Sea for the first time, they realized they could float. Dressed in long sleeves and long pants out of respect for their Muslim faith, they embraced the water without fear. Afghanistan is a landlocked country, and there was joyous laughter as the girls experienced a new world beyond war.

Our trip continued by train to Rome, where we visited a famous mosque, and there, the grand mufti, the ranking interpreter of Muslim law in Italy, presented me with a copy of the Holy Qur'an—a gesture of respect for removing these girls from a war-torn region to visit another part of the word. Catholic cardinal Renato Martino also invited us to the Vatican with interfaith respect; just as the farmers had recited in Mir Bacha Kot, we are all daughters and sons of Abraham. I love that.

About ten years later, I wondered what had become of Fawad. Our staff looked into it and reported that he was now living in London and that, thanks to his experience with Roots of Peace, he had been invited to join Arsenal, one of England's oldest and most accomplished soccer clubs. And, get this—he was driving a specially designed Mercedes-Benz with one good leg.

Fawad reconnected with Kyleigh on their thirtieth birthdays, twelve years after their first meeting in the Red Cross clinic in Kabul—two travelers on life's path with the same date of birth but different destinies, and guided by the same miraculous powers.

On our return from Afghanistan on August 17, 2005, we were excited to reunite with our friends who had actively supported the mission of a mother and daughter flying to Afghanistan to heal the wounds of war. As a divine blessing for our protection prior to our departure to Kabul, Erika Hills, worried about our safety, had placed on my shoulders a *milagro* necklace from Latin America with beautiful orange, coral, and silver hearts. Erika had hosted a luncheon with her husband, Austin, and Mike Grgich, and they toasted to our success with their own Private Reserve bottle from Grgich Hills Estate. Nobel Laureate Jody Williams joined us in Erika and Austin's Napa Valley backyard, as we planted a symbolic grapevine and white rose in tribute to our mines-to-vines initiative.

On the morning of our return, Erika called me, saying with her famously thick Austrian accent, "Welcome home from your peace mission, darling!" Dori Bonn, her best friend, was volunteering in our Roots of Peace offices, and we were both thrilled when Erika offered to drive down from Napa Valley to take us to lunch in Marin County to celebrate our success—just the three of us! Speaking to her at 11:30 A.M., we told her to take her time driving, as we had lots of work to do after my trip to Afghanistan.

Hour after hour, we waited. Finally, we received a call from her husband, Austin Hills, who told us that Erika would not be joining us for lunch. Shrugging our shoulders in puzzlement, we both enthusiastically said, "Well, let's make it tomorrow instead!" There was silence on the phone. Austin continued with a broken voice, "Erika will never be joining us for lunch again. She died in a car crash en route along the Silverado Trail." A hitch on a truck carrying several tons of metal had come loose, and the heavy equipment for excavating a wine cave had cascaded across the lanes, killing her instantly. Like the late Princess Diana, Erika had left two boys behind after the car crash: Austin Jr. and Justin.

At sunset, we meandered on our weak legs into St. Raphael's Church—named after the archangel associated with healing—in San Rafael to pray for our dearest friend, whose voice had been so alive just a few hours before. At that same moment, a Latino family walked into the chapel to the accompaniment of beautiful guitar music, there to witness a baptism. Sunlight filled the altar. A new child had been born. Such is the circle of life, and I am reminded every day I do the work of Roots of Peace that while people pass away—in car accidents, from senseless landmines—our job as humans is to turn that pain into hope and use the needless tragedy as motivation in our quest for peace worldwide.

A few days later, Grace Cathedral in San Francisco was filled with nearly one thousand mourners; Dori and I were Erika's only two friends invited to speak at her funeral. Like the candle in the wind, another extraordinary light was extinguished.

Somehow, we all managed to find our center of gravity. Kyleigh passionately inspired the youth of California to carry on in the spirit of Erika Hills. Within a few months, she and her Roots of Peace team had once again collected millions of pennies, this time to build a school for the children of Mir Bacha Kot. I called a friend, Shamim Jawad, wife of

Afghanistan's ambassador to the United States, to tell her of the commitment Kyleigh had made to build a school, and Shamim offered to join the effort.

Construction of the school could not begin immediately because fields surrounding the construction site were still infested with landmines planted by Soviet soldiers after their invasion in 1979 and later by the Taliban. After weeks of landmine clearance, however, the day finally came to begin building.

In 2006, Shamim and I flew to Kabul. Arriving at night, we were met by our escorts—gun-toting bodyguards who took us to their armored cars and drove us to Mir Bacha Kot. It was our dream to watch the sunrise over the Shomali Plain, and we set our alarms for 4 A.M. to drive for one hour in the dark to witness the sunrise over the vineyards. When we arrived, the dew was on the green grape leaves, and the scent of fresh red grapes filled the morning air. Truly, it was a breath of heaven, as these grapes had been grown on a former minefield. It takes approximately four years for a grapevine to grow, and the fields had been demined in 2002. The land was ripe for a harvest of hope.

Later in the day, Shamim and I knelt down in the dirt and laid the cornerstone of the new school along with two American pennies, an admission that our tiny efforts were no more than a mere two cents for peace. The Afghans unveiled the name of the school—the Kyleigh Kühn School—which brought tears to my eyes. It is unusual in Afghanistan to name a school after an American, but the genuine efforts of a young woman inspired the minister of education to make an exception. Before the day got too hot, we drove to Shakardara, the name of which translates into "Sugar Mountain," to witness the important demining work that continued in the field.

Brave deminers wearing heavy suits defied the sweltering heat and began to meticulously comb the earth inch by inch. We were taken to a remote hillside and told to be quiet. The deminers proceeded to a grave-yard where fresh flowers had been left by local villagers. Puzzled, I asked why they were disturbing the peace in the cemetery. With downcast eyes, the Afghan deminers told us that the respected place where the dead were laid to rest had been deliberately mined by the enemy, knowing that the loved ones of the deceased would insist on bringing flowers, even through a minefield. Absolutely quiet, I watched the demining team lay dynamite from a distance. Three! Two! One! *Blast!* Those who had been laid to rest died twice—once when their hearts stopped, and once when their graves were disturbed by the blast of demining.

On one close call, a deminer was excavating a landmine in an open field where children were playing at a safe distance, and I was quietly watching over his shoulder. As he began to remove the dirt while cameras were rolling, numbers on the unexploded remnant of war were uncovered: MS3. Puzzled, I turned to see an expression of horror on the face of the deminer, who ordered an immediate evacuation. The MS3 is a pressure-release mine; when five kilograms or more of pressure is placed on it, then removed, it triggers. The children ran fast—away from where we were standing. Fortunately, the MS3 did not detonate, and our lives were spared.

This was a very real moment—one that deminers face daily around the world. While all precautions were taken, there are seeds of terror in the soil that one may not anticipate. And so goes life.

Shamim had become a good friend. We may have come from opposite sides of the world, but we shared an appreciation for the critical importance of education in young people's lives and were both outraged that during the years of oppressive Taliban rule, the young women of Afghanistan had been forbidden to go to school. Music had also been forbidden, as were dancing and books—it had been a culture of "no" for women, and for young girls in particular, who were denied any childhood dreams of a bright future and any resources that could get them there.

In May 2007, the *Queen Mary 2* offered to host a Roots of Peace cruise to further our efforts to raise awareness and funds to achieve our goal to turn mines to vines. Pat Geiger, our children's teacher, championed our cause to her travel agency, owned by Rotarians Carlos and K-K Afre, which agreed to host a special transatlantic cruise to England in support of Princess Diana's vision. It had been a decade since Diana's tragic death in Paris, when we commemorated her legacy for landmine removal. Her Majesty Queen Noor and singer-songwriter Judy Collins joined me on board the vessel in New York Harbor. As three proud American women, we entered the glass elevator down to the dining room and glanced at the representation of another woman, the Statue of Liberty, as we proudly carried our own torch! "All rise for the Queen!" exclaimed the captain, as the doors opened and we set sail for new horizons in mine-removal action. Ambassador Said Jawad and his wife, Shamim, joined us for five days, as we shared stories of Afghanistan to inspire both passengers and crew.

The following year, in October 2008, we met again, this time for the inauguration of yet another project: the ten-classroom Kyleigh Kühn School. In that first year alone, enrollment grew from 20 to more than 600 students. Over the years, there were many dedication ceremonies, and one of the highlights was the 2009 visit of Major General Barbara J. Faulkenberry, one of the highest-ranking females in the US Air Force. Faulkenberry had an avid interest in landmine issues and, thanks to an introduction by Nannette Griswold of the International Women's Forum, she had agreed to fly 1,800 miles from Baghdad to Kabul for the inauguration.

Faulkenberry's staff called to request exact geographical coordinates, as the school was not clearly visible in its remote region of the Shomali Plain. I was with students inside the school when we heard the whir of helicopter blades rotating overhead in the hot morning air. We ran outside and looked up to see helicopters flanked by drones scouring the sky for enemy missiles. The noise was deafening.

Just then, a convoy of about twenty diesel-powered Mine Resistant Ambush Protected vehicles approached the schoolyard. The MRAPs zigzagged back and forth, and it seemed clear that the drivers could not find the tiny road that served as the entrance to the school grounds. Not one to be intimidated by mere twenty-three-ton armored monster trucks, I walked to the edge of the road and opened my beige vest. "See?" the gesture was intended to convey. "No bombs." During the years of conflict, suicide bombers had posed as innocent mothers, and I prayed that the US military would realize I wasn't one of them.

The convoy took my signal and entered the schoolyard. A soldier in US military uniform stuck his head out of the tank.

"Identify yourself!" he shouted.

"My name is Heidi Kühn," I yelled out. "I'm the CEO of Roots of Peace."

There was some discussion from within the tank, and then Faulkenberry emerged with a smile on her face and, waving me over, invited me to join her in the MRAP. I climbed up the side of the tank, put on a flak jacket, positioned earphones on my head, and off we went. My daughter, Kyleigh, standing near the entrance to the school as I passed by, perched in the tank's gun turret, looked at me with her mouth open and shook her head slowly back and forth. No ordinary housewife.

Once the soldiers secured the location, Faulkenberry and I walked into the school, and students presented her with bouquets of colorful fresh flowers and greeted her in English: "Welcome, General Faulkenberry. Our Afghan-American school was built with pennies from children all over the world."

The students then sang a few traditional folk songs and did a show-and-tell of drawings they'd made depicting their lives in Mir Bacha Kot. Mohammad Sharif Osmani, formerly a taxi driver and now Roots of Peace country director for Afghanistan, stepped forward and welcomed Faulkenberry with a polite bow. The day went perfectly, a fitting dedication.

During this visit to Afghanistan, one incident bears mentioning because it speaks to the trust and loyalty our friends have shown over the years regarding the work of Roots of Peace. When we could not make payroll for our three hundred employees in Kandahar because of a delay in the transfer of funds from the United States, I asked Bill Murray, founder of the Bank of Marin, for help. Bill had been my supporter for years—he had originally sponsored me as a Rotary Youth Ambassador to Utsunomiya, Japan, in 1975, and nominated me to membership in the Rotary Club of San Rafael in 1997.

Now he made yet another offer of support by proposing to approve a loan from his bank if my family and I agreed to use our own home as collateral. It was the quickest way of getting us the $300,000 we needed, and he would personally shepherd the loan through to approval. We agreed, because the stakes were very high. There were lives at risk, and our organization's credibility was on the line if we could not make payroll in time. Offering our home as collateral was the least we could do to solve the problem.

As effective a solution as this was, the other Bank of Marin directors were opposed. Risking the bank's money to help a charitable program in war-torn Afghanistan, with or without collateral, was beyond the usual scope of the bank's activities. The directors tried to dissuade me, saying the loan was risky and I could lose my beloved family home.

"Your people need to find some other way to solve your cash-flow problems," one board member told me. "Forget the whole thing, and go back to your life as a mother and a wife." Just the kind of chauvinistic comment I loved to hear. "Your home was given to you by your grand-mother—why take such risks?" he argued.

"I'm willing to take the risk," I told him, barely controlling my out-rage, "because our employees are taking even greater risks trying to restore their country despite threats from the Taliban. Our employees are loyal workers, and if they are not paid on time, they won't be able to feed their children. I need to maintain their trust, and I'm ready to take the responsibility to do that."

Bill, visibly moved by my forceful rebuttal, made the extraordinary move of personally backing the loan. The funds were released, and the Roots of Peace cash-flow crisis was solved. Eventually, we did repay the $300,000 loan against our family home—a happy ending to a precarious dilemma.

Just as I was at the brink of giving up, my intrepid spirit was once again met with an unexpected blessing. In 2006, I delivered a passion-ate speech at the annual meeting of Conservation International, and a woman who had once worked for Hewlett-Packard's HP Foundation, which had funded my initial business plan, was in the audience and heard my words. Her name was Ruth Norris, and she had recently gone to work for Jeff Skoll, a successful Silicon Valley leader who had launched the innovative Skoll Award for Social Entrepreneurship. And, while my cause was a long shot, Ruth wanted to put my name in as a candidate among a select group of entrepreneurs whose innovations have had a significant, proven impact on some of the world's most pressing problems.

By investing in an organization when its initiative is ripe for accelerated and scaled adoption, the Skoll Award helps unleash the full potential and reach of social entrepreneurs. "The Skoll Award is for those visionaries who are a spokesperson on their issue, who have taken great risks," Ruth told me. "I think you would be a solid candidate based on your clear and unwavering focus on your mission of eradicating landmines and planting peace."

Much to my surprise, Roots of Peace was selected as the recipient charity of this distinguished award. The monetary value of the grant was $750,000, a catalytic investment that allowed us to rise to the next level of social impact. Actors Sir Ben Kingsley and Robert Redford personally presented this special award to me in the Nelson Mandela Room at the University of Oxford's Saïd Business School.

I was humbled and honored to stand in their presence and receive the award on behalf of those living in war-torn lands who had no voices. The evening celebration was hosted in Christ Church College's Dining Hall at the university, where parts of the Harry Potter franchise had been filmed, and the evening was truly filled with magic beyond my wildest imagination. Stained glass windows reflected the vibrant heritage of those visionaries who had dined there in years past, including Lewis

Carroll, author of *Alice's Adventures in Wonderland*. I felt as if I were peering through a magical looking glass at a new future of possibilities supporting my vision for planting the roots of peace.

The following year, in November 2007, we returned to Afghanistan to visit the school in Mir Bacha Kot, this time accompanied by actress Diane Baker, whose illustrious career included such films as *The Diary of Anne Frank* and *The Silence of the Lambs*. Diane and I had met at the KPIX television studios in San Francisco in 2003, when we'd both been scheduled for interviews. That day had been a difficult one for me, as my mother was in the hospital, and I was clutching my rosary beads in one hand while carrying in the other three inert landmines to use as props during the interview. Accidentally, the landmines slipped from my arms, and technicians ducked in an involuntary reflex on seeing bombs hit the hard wood floor.

"I'm so sorry," I said quickly. "They're inactive—for demonstration purposes only. They were given to me by the US Department of State to explain the impact of landmines on innocent victims . . ."

Diane heard my explanation and volunteered to hold the landmines for me during the taping. Without thinking, I also handed her the rosary beads. I took my place on the set, the cameras rolled, and I described for the reporter what it had been like walking across a minefield in Croatia while holding my thirteen-year-old daughter's hand. Diane was visibly moved by the story, and after the interview, she asked what it would take for her to be allowed to join Roots of Peace.

"Not much," I said. "In fact, you just qualified. Welcome aboard."

Two months later, we flew together to Croatia, where we met with President Stjepan Mesić, and afterward, Diane and I inspected fields that had been demined by Roots of Peace. The progress was impressive, as one field after another was freed of live landmines.

Some years later, we again traveled together to Afghanistan, this time to visit the Kyleigh Kühn School in Mir Bacha Kot. We flew from Kabul to Mazar-e Sharif. Then we drove to the provinces of Samangan and Balkh. We arrived bearing gifts from America—a group of women back home in California had knitted sweaters, hats, and gloves to distribute to the Afghan children at the school, warm clothing that would protect children living in the mountainous regions of a country where winter temperatures frequently dropped below freezing. When we arrived, we noted forty or so armed Afghan guards standing on rooftops around the school, protecting us while we distributed large cardboard boxes of hand-knitted items to hundreds of young people in the community.

From the school, Diane and I drove to a local women's prison, where we were given permission to meet the twenty or so women living in the prison's two small rooms. Whatever their presumed offenses, no one deserved to live in such conditions. The prisoners shared one toilet—a hole in the ground—and the stench of urine was nauseating. Between the two rooms, there was a tiny courtyard, where sunlight penetrated for a few hours each day. Among the prisoners were four small children who greeted us with soiled stuffed animals and broken dolls.

"Why are these children in prison?" I demanded.

Through an interpreter, a guard explained that if they had been left outside, the children would have been stoned by their communities for the crimes of their parents. Keeping them with their mothers in prison was saving their lives.

"And the women prisoners," I said, "what were their crimes?"

The guard nudged me with the tip of his gun toward the second room, where, behind a filthy curtain, I found a newborn child in the arms of its mother. The child, only a few hours old, lay wrapped in blood-stained sheets. Through a translator, the mother told me she had been raped by her uncle on the eve of her wedding night. The husband's family had claimed it was her fault for being so beautiful and irresistible in the eyes of a family member, and she had been imprisoned for this "crime." Nine months after her imprisonment, only a few hours before we had arrived, she had given birth.

She gently placed her newborn in my arms and whispered, "Please take the baby away. Take her out of prison."

The three of us wept for some time, but I handed the baby back and hugged the mother, and the young woman wailed as prison guards escorted me and Diane out of the dark, dingy room. We walked out of the prison with our chests pounding. I will never forget the piercing sound of that mother's cries. They are forever etched in my heart.

Some time later, Roots of Peace began construction of another school, this one in the Bam Saray area of Bamyan. (The name, which translates as "the place of shining light," alludes to the quality of light at its high elevation.) This was the region where, in 2001, the Taliban had dynamited ancient and very sacred giant Buddha mountain sculptures.

When construction was finished, the country's first female governor, Dr. Habiba Sarabi, led the inauguration ceremony. This school, too, had been built with millions of pennies collected by Kyleigh and her schoolmates. Kyleigh and I looked at each other and smiled, remembering our friends Walid and Nadia, who had been so terrified of reprisals following the September 11 tragedy that they had scissored the word *Afghan* out of the menus of their restaurant in San Rafael.

Over the years since that inauguration, the school has received many distinguished visitors: diplomats, ambassadors, Hollywood stars, news anchors, and army generals, among others. Princess Homaira, granddaughter of Mohammed Zahir Shah, the last king of Afghanistan, had hosted a fundraiser in Rome to purchase the school desks and chairs. That event was organized by Flavia Taggiasco, the CNN producer who had covered our Roots of Peace mines-to-vines story in 2004 in Croatia. After her report, Flavia became a dedicated supporter of our cause and enlisted donations from more than four hundred of her friends and contacts in Italy, including American-born actress Sydne Rome, who had many connections. Sydne acted in Italian films and TV series, and her star quality cast a bright light on our efforts to eradicate landmines.

We visited the school several times over the next few years, and on one trip, my friend Shamim Jawad, wife of Afghanistan's ambassador to the United States, proposed that we schedule a meeting with President Hamid Karzai. Thanks to Shamim's government contacts, the visit was approved, and we arrived at the president's office with a box of fresh pomegranates harvested from fields cultivated by Roots of Peace near Kandahar, the city where Karzai was born. I'll never forget how his eyes lit up with surprise on opening the box of ripe, beautiful fruit. All his life, he had only seen pomegranates of different sizes packed loosely in burlap sacks, where they bounced around and bruised. The Roots of Peace pomegranates were large, uniformly sized, bursting with juice, and packed professionally in a grocery-style box.

"This reminds me of my childhood," he said, eyeing the fruit with a smile. "We used to put a straw into a pomegranate and drink the juice. It's the best taste in the world. And did you know that pomegranates are the world's oldest fruit? They are mentioned in the Bible."

We described for him the "economics of peace" that was the foundation of our work: funding demining companies like MAG, the HALO Trust, CROMAC, and Quadro to demine fields, then having Roots of Peace staff determine the most productive use of the land and train farmers to prosper.

"Congratulations," Karzai told us. "You have successfully transformed bombs into pomegranates!"

CHAPTER NINE

PEACE, LOVE & WAR

He who sows the ground with care and diligence
acquires a greater stock of merit than is gained
by the repetition of ten thousand prayers.

—ZOROASTER, FOUNDER OF ZOROASTRIANISM

More bombs were dropped on Vietnam during the war than all the bombs in Europe and throughout the Pacific during World War II combined. As a young girl in the 1960s, my family and I watched the evening news on television and shuddered at newsreel footage showing the consequences of this deadly and inhuman practice. Each night, renowned broadcast journalist Walter Cronkite announced the body count: so many hundreds of caskets waiting to be transported back to grieving families in America; so many thousands of Vietnamese, young and old, with missing limbs or dead. Each night, before sleep, I prayed that I might play some small part in helping alleviate the suffering.

If someone were to trace the roots of my own commitment to peace, they would have to reach back to my days as a student of political economics at the University of California, Berkeley, during the 1970s, where the movement against the war in Vietnam had drawn large numbers of young people. UC Berkeley was also where I met Gary, my future husband and steadfast partner in Roots of Peace. We began as teenage idealists with a hazy vision of peace and found ourselves years later as seasoned pros with a finely tuned vision of what to do.

Along the way, we learned that there was an obscene number of active landmines in Vietnam. In just one province, Quảng Tri, which straddled the Demilitarized Zone, or DMZ, and is located in the Central Highlands between Hanoi and Ho Chi Minh City (Saigon), more than 80 percent of the land was still riddled with landmines, UXOs, and cluster munition, totaling in the millions. The longer Gary and I worked in the anti-landmine movement, the more disturbed we became about who the majority of victims of these landmines were: not soldiers, but innocent children and poor farmers. The injustice of that rang in our heads.

Often, we felt terribly isolated in our work. What had happened to the peace movement? Where was the spirit of the 1970s? It seemed peace and love had faded into history. Despite some successes with generous donations, it continued to be an uphill battle to raise funds for Roots of Peace, and we were still so far from our goal. The history of social action was clear to us; we knew how often social entrepreneurs hit the wall. It is exhausting to constantly speak about your cause, raise money, and organize, especially when your passionate ideas fall on deaf ears.

In 2007, I was honored to receive the prestigious Jacqueline Kennedy Onassis Award for Outstanding Public Service Benefiting Local

Communities, sponsored by the Jefferson Awards Foundation (now called Multiplying Good). Yet I did not want to simply gather medals and keep them on my shelf. I wanted them to count!

Then came one of those serendipitous moments, which I choose to call grace, when the opportunity came to implement Roots of Peace in Vietnam. It began with an invitation to attend the Global Philanthropy Forum in Silicon Valley in 2009, following the Skoll World Forum in Oxford.

While there, I lobbied everyone I met to support turning mines to vines, emphasizing the value and rewards of replacing the scourge of land-mines with bountiful agricultural crops. Many people there had heard about Roots of Peace, but few thought it had much hope for success. The sheer number of landmines around the world was too great, they warned, and the cost too exorbitant. Our prospects at this philanthropy forum didn't look good.

Exhausted from days of walking and talking and trying to persuade someone, anyone, to help our cause, I was sitting at the back of a confer-ence room listening to one more speaker lecture about one more point of social entrepreneurship. There were several hundred people in the room. I needed to be alone and had picked a seat at the back, hoping to avoid having to speak to anyone. Sitting next to me was a woman with a sore throat. Although she could barely talk, she asked me what I did. Normally, I'm happy to describe my work, but that day, I was spent and reluctant to engage. Besides, it pained me to hear her crackling voice. I happened to have with me a cup of hot tea with lemon and honey. I handed it to her, smiled and turned away. The woman was persistent.

"What does that mean," she asked, "'CEO, Roots of Peace'?" She pointed to my name tag.

"My organization turn mines to vines," I said, and I gave her a brief overview about clearing landmines and planting high-yield agricultural produce. Her eyes widened with interest. She asked a flurry of questions.

"Could this model be replicated anywhere in the world?" she asked.

"Yes," I said. "We've implemented our program in a few countries now. There's a long way to go."

The woman coughed—the tea was helping, but not that much—and asked, "Would you be interested in demining and replanting Vietnam?"

I was convinced this was futile small talk but humored her.

"Working in Vietnam has been my dream since my student days at Cal Berkeley," I told her. "I've always believed in the idea of peace—but I get restless when people only talk about it in theory." I needed to rest and hoped that the indirect jab would dissuade her from further chitchat. She looked at me expectantly, with unblinking eyes. *OK*, I thought, *I'll give it a few more minutes.*

"The peace movement needs to be grounded in something tangible," I said. "Roots of Peace does that by removing landmines and planting valuable crops as a starting point for a country's renewed future."

The mystery woman and I exchanged business cards, and we promised to speak again a few days later, after her voice returned. To be honest, I didn't think about our conversation again; there had been so many just like it at the conference. I had a purse full of business cards. There was a little interest from a few foundations, but human nature being what it is, I knew better than to expect much to come of it.

The phone rang the following Monday morning.

"Hello, this is Tory Dietel Hopps," said the voice at the other end of the line. "Do you remember me? I'd like to discuss funding your program in Vietnam."

"Yes, Mrs. Dietel Hopps," I said, vaguely remembering the voice. "Can you hold for a moment?" If this was real, I wanted Gary on the call. He was the genius of the business side of Roots of Peace. I waved at him to pick up the extension phone.

"Hello, Mrs. Dietel Hopps. This is Gary Kühn," he began. "How can we help you?"

"Actually, Mr. and Mrs. Kühn," she replied. "I would like to help *you*."

By the end of the day, we had a donor (until now anonymous) who believed in Roots of Peace enough to provide $450,000 to begin demining Quảng Tri Province.

And people wonder why I pray on Muslim, Buddhist, and Catholic beads.

For our newly funded campaign, we decided Gary should first fly to Vietnam with our agricultural experts to assess the land for its potential to grow crops. After conducting an initial investigation in Quảng Tri and speaking with local government authorities, he identified the first step: Obtain approval from the Communist government in Hanoi. This was the biggest hurdle for any American nongovernmental organization—it was essential to gain the government's trust if we were to be granted the necessary legal documentation and permits.

On May 16, 2008, our son Tucker graduated with a degree in political science from the University of San Francisco.[7] Tucker has blue eyes, blond hair, and an outgoing personality. He approached me and Gary and candidly asked whether he could submit his résumé to work with Roots of Peace in Vietnam. As his mother, my first impulse was to tell him to

---

7. This happened to be on the same day that news broke of Robert Mondavi's death. Robert was our first donor, and he is deeply missed.

run in the opposite direction. The work was dangerous, even life-threatening. I had already brought two of our children on missions, and all I could hear was my own conscience chastising me, "What kind of mother are you, endangering your family with your crazy visions—sending your son, an American boy, to wage a campaign in a country devastated by America just a few decades before?"

I had to bite my tongue. It was all I could do to keep from telling Tucker, "Follow in your father's footsteps, not mine. Be safe. Go to graduate school. Do anything, but don't do this. Our work isn't glamorous. It's deadly."

That evening, Gary came to me and said, "Tucker's fairly obsessed about it." He laughed and added with a wry smile, "I wonder where he got that kind of fierce focus. It seems to me he's doing what we always wanted him to do—following his heart no matter where it leads. We should be proud of him and trust him enough to let him go."

It didn't take long for me to see the writing on the wall. "I give in," I said.

It turned out that Gary had slightly ulterior motives—all for the good of the project, of course. He wanted Tucker to travel with him to Vietnam so that our son could learn and eventually oversee the program himself.

"I think Tucker just might have what it takes to guide our organization there to the next level," Gary said.

And so my boy, the apple of my eye, would travel to Vietnam with us. In a sense, my college dreams of peacemaking were being realized by my own son, who was setting out to take his place on the front line for peace. It was time to pass the torch to the next generation.

I had learned from my husband about the importance of taking care of the business side of our project. As a business, our first priority in Vietnam was the organizational aspect of opening a branch of Roots of Peace. After that, Gary would groom Tucker for his future role as our country director. The system they worked out was to schedule daily Skype calls. That way Gary, could guide Tucker through the next step, which was to hire a Vietnamese team to assist him in implementation of the Roots of Peace program.

After the horrors of the war, which had killed three million of their people, Vietnamese government officials were understandably skeptical of another American intervention, even from an NGO like ours. But Tucker's youthful exuberance, his personality, and the respectful way he researched traditional agricultural practices helped him quickly build friendships and trust among Vietnamese partners. To demonstrate his solidarity with them, he even learned to participate in *"Mot, hai, ba, vo!,"* a popular custom while drinking beer over ice. Eventually, the government approved an initial project in Bình Phước.

Tucker was twenty-five when he arrived in Bình Phước to assess the planting of cashews, a lucrative crop on the international market. With his father's assistance, Tucker introduced a new form of planting that involved placing cacao trees between the rows of cashew trees. This method, called intercropping, was an innovation that enabled local farmers to double or triple their income by expanding production while also promoting greater biodiversity. Neighboring farmers visited the demonstration plots and quickly adopted the technique. The demand for cacao was high, and soon international companies were arriving to negotiate purchases of crops, and the farmers' standard of living began to rise.

In 2010, I first met Huynh, the boy with no face, through our work in Quảng Trị, and he described how one day, in the summer of 1995, he was playing with his twin brother, Hoa, in a field adjoining their home. Nearby, a neighbor was digging for scrap metal with a shovel. Like other people in this part of Vietnam, the neighbor was so poor that pennies earned from selling wartime scrap metal were the only means available to him for feeding his children. The neighbor stuck his shovel into the ground.

Boom!

He was blown into a thousand pieces. Huynh's twin brother, Hoa, lay on the ground with an arm missing and shrapnel wounds all over his body. Huynh's face was destroyed by the blast. What remained, even after months of healing, were his eyes and holes for his mouth and nose. It was a cruel mask for a child to wear for the rest of his life.

In 1998, a Swedish businessman heard about Huynh's condition and decided to make it his mission to restore the boy's face. Vietnam did not have many qualified plastic surgeons at that time, so the businessman searched for a doctor in the United States who would accept the task.

A specialist in Boston offered to help, and with funding from the Swedish businessman, Huynh was flown to the United States. In due course, doctors were able to sufficiently reconstruct Huynh's mouth so that he could speak, though his face remains radically scarred.

That's the kind of reality we live with every day at Roots of Peace. The work to eradicate landmines cannot be done fast enough, and we all worked hard to get the program going.

We called the program SHADE, Sustainable Horticulture and Agriculture Development, and by 2011 we had trained nearly 1,000 farmers in eighty-eight villages to grow cacao intercropped with cashews, which substantially increased their income. We contemplated how to best improve the track record set by the SHADE project and came up with the concept of Cacao Clubs. The best farmers became Cacao Club Leaders, and they were invited to attend train-the-trainer courses, after which we approved them to train other farmers. USDA Rural Development, impressed by this mentoring system, provided funds for its expansion.

Cacao Club Leaders trained thousands of farmers in intercrop planting, and within a matter of months, they in turn had planted an astonishing 251,000 trees and increased their individual incomes by as much as 250 percent. Building on this success, we transitioned the leadership of the Vietnamese-led cacao program to major international partners along with local community businesses. These partners continued to provide additional technical assistance for a time and purchased the cacao crops at fair international market prices. We have seen that Roots of Peace farmers who continue to take care of cacao orchards have a more stable source of income and become better off by selling their beans to domestic cocoa-processing companies.

In 2011, Roots of Peace expanded the SHADE program to include black pepper, a crop that has high value in international markets. One story among many illustrates just how important these programs became for local farmers. Nguyen Dinh Thu was a Vietnamese farmer living in Quảng Tri. While working in the fields one day as a teenager, he saw a shiny object unearthed after a heavy rain. When he tried to excavate it, the UXO exploded.

When Nguyen woke up covered in blood, he realized that he no longer had any hands and was also missing part of his arms. Though no war was being fought in his country, he became a victim of war that day. He survived, but his life was changed forever. After several surgeries, he had no option but to return home and farm the same land where he had been maimed. Despite his injuries, he forged ahead and struggled to farm without arms.

As Dinh Thu watched his friends get married and move on with their lives, he decided not to be held back by the challenges in his own life. He started walking dozens of kilometers each day, and then he started riding a bike—all with no hands. He made a living traveling around on his bike, trading goods of all kinds.

In 2001, Dinh Thu married Mai. They had a son in 2002, and the couple worked hard, growing beans, pepper, rice, taro, and other plants and raising pigs and chickens to create a stable source of income for the family.

When Roots of Peace came to the Vĩnh Linh District of Quảng Trị, Dinh Thu registered for the program. He joined the training courses and worked to learn the new science and apply the new techniques to his garden. When he joined, he said, "I see a good future. The monetary support of Roots of Peace is not much, but the education focused on science and technology is more practical and useful."

Roots of Peace invited Dinh Thu to join the SHADE program. Our staff found and cleared eleven more UXOs from his land, then helped him plant pepper vines. In time, Dinh Thu saw his pepper orchard go from the brink of collapse to a thriving enterprise. He became a Black Pepper Club Leader, grew prosperous, and became a role model for other farmers in his area devastated by landmines. Under his guidance, many other Quảng Trị farmers also became well-to-do, and Tucker, Vietnam's Roots of Peace country director, was celebrated as a local hero. More than 250,000 cacao trees were planted under Tucker's leadership, and that success opened the door for Roots of Peace to expand the SHADE project into other provinces.

Once the program in Dinh Thu's area got going and the techniques introduced were proven to work, he and other families in the village, armed with their new knowledge, were excited and ready to expand production. They now knew how to dig trenches against flooding, plant and take care of the peppers, protect the peppers from diseases, and package the peppers for sale. He and other farmers had grown the confidence to bet on their own businesses, and they started to flourish.

In Dinh Thu's own words, "I hope that after Roots of Peace's help, my children's lives will be better than mine."

The history of the Vĩnh Linh District was an eye-opener for us. The Vĩnh Mốc tunnels had been at the front line of the war. More than 600 Vietnamese families had hand-dug them beneath the earth to escape bombings during the war, and seventeen babies were born underground during those years when families hid from the enemy. When they emerged to the world above, they found that 80 percent of their land had been contaminated by deadly explosive ordnance.

Years later, when I first visited Vietnam, I decided I needed to empathize as much as sympathize. One of my first acts was to crawl through the narrow, dank, and dark tunnels of Vĩnh Mốc, as many of the people I was now working with had done during the war. It was summer, the air was hot and humid, and it was difficult to breathe. As I wormed my way through the tunnels, I tried to imagine the ground above being pummeled by the bombs that kept families underground for years.

Before the devastation of the war, Vĩnh Linh had grown the finest pepper vines in the country. Tucker negotiated draft agreements for

Roots of Peace to facilitate the removal of landmines and plant pepper vines across the province, a program estimated to improve, initially, the lives of more than 2,000 farmers.

During my travels around the country, I met many more incredible survivors. I visited a mushroom farmer who had stepped on a mine and lost both legs up to his thighs. He had a bright smile and used his arms, his torso, and two wooden blocks to pull himself around as he showed me his high-quality mushroom farm, which had benefited from intercropping pepper vines. His family was clearly proud of him, his accomplishments, and their friendship with our Roots of Peace staff.

I also met Dao Ba Tranh, another victim of the landmine scourge in Vietnam. As a young boy in Quảng Tri, he grew up a world apart from me, listening to the sounds of bombs dropping on his village rather than the music of the 1960s I and my friends were dancing to.

Dao's child lived in the same hamlet where he had grown up, and he and his family knew there was thunder in the ground. His wife choked back tears as she explained, "In the morning, my child went out into our fields to tend buffalo with his two best friends. I was looking forward to seeing him in the late afternoon for dinner. Suddenly, I heard a big explosion. Then, some minutes later, my son's dead body was carried home."

The Vietnam War will not end until all explosive remnants of war are removed.

As a mother and grandmother from the peace-and-love generation at UC Berkeley during the 1970s, I call on my friends who stood for these basic human principles that defined our generation. May we remember our own generation's roots of peace.

In 2015, Cardinal Peter Kodwo Appiah Turkson, president of the Vatican's Pontifical Council for Justice and Peace, sent Monsignor Paul Phan, his personal emissary, to inspect the minefields of Quảng Tri. During the Vietnam War, Phan's father had served in the former DMZ as chief of police. Phan, the oldest of eight children, recalled hearing bombs falling near his home when he was a child. He had been a promising student and athlete, but his mother had died giving birth to her next child, and Phan had been left to take care of the family while his father earned a living. Phan, who joined the local monastery, remembered seeing two of his fellow monastics walking to church, stepping on a landmine, and being blown to bits.

One morning, during his visit in 2016, he asked me to join him on a drive someplace special. He had a surprise for me, he said, from His Holiness Pope Francis. We arrived at Ha Lang District, where I saw a beautiful basilica, an enormous Catholic church, under construction. This one sat alongside the burnt remnants of a smaller church, which had clearly been destroyed during the Vietnam War.

"This is Our Lady of La Vang," Phan said. "In 1798, people from this district fled to the forest to avoid religious persecution. There, they fell gravely ill. Then the Blessed Mother appeared with a message of healing and love, instructing them to seek out the La Vang herb, which healed them of their sickness—much as you are healing the land now, two hundred years later."

"In 1998, Pope John Paul II had expressed a desire to complete construction of this basilica," Phan announced to me, "as a commemoration of two hundred years since that vision of the Blessed Mother. And the Vatican is praying for all that you are doing for my country to bring forth the removal of landmines and sow the seeds of love in the healing spirit of Our Lady of La Vang."

I've learned that sometimes the only response to good news is to be thankful—really, really thankful. We humbly bowed our heads and prayed for healing of the land at the foot of the tree.

The vision of going from mines to vines and turning swords into plowshares has gone full circle, validated by the many good souls who have furthered the work of Roots of Peace. Dr. Emma Farr Rawlings and her husband, Jim Farrell, joined us to see the fruits of our labor. The next year, they nominated me for the first Earth Ethics Prize, presented by Claes Nobel, a descendant of Alfred Nobel, who established the Nobel prizes. His son, Marcus Nobel, joined me in the fields of Quảng Tri to detonate a landmine—a powerful statement from the family of the man who had invented dynamite, which in turn enabled development of more destructive bombs; now, here we were, working with Roots of Peace to detonate mines for peace and safety.

CHAPTER TEN

THE ABRAHAMIC PATH

They are the true yogis who, by comparison with their own selves,
see the true equality of all beings
in both their happiness and their distress.

—Bhagavad Gita 6.32

In June 2010, Jerry White, executive director of the Survivor Corps (formerly the Landmine Survivors Network), who had been with us since the launch of Roots of Peace in 1998, called to say he had just arrived in San Francisco from Washington, DC, and that I should stay put and not leave my San Rafael office: He had something important to tell me. Over the years we'd known each other, I discovered it was a good idea to always do whatever Jerry White told me to do, so I canceled everything I had scheduled for the rest of the day and sat in my office, waiting for him to show up.

An hour or so later, Jerry arrived in a rented car and walked in, smiling like the Cheshire Cat.

"Heidi," he said, "I want you to fly with me to Tel Aviv."

"What do you have in mind?" I asked, pretending to be indifferent to the idea. Inside, I was jumping up and down. Tel Aviv was not just the second-largest city in Israel and the country's economic and technological center, but, more important for me personally, it was only a one-hour drive from Jerusalem. All my life, I'd wanted to go on pilgrimage to the birthplace of my faith. Bringing Roots of Peace to the Holy Land would be a dream come true.

"There's a young man there I'd like you to meet," Jerry said. "His name is Daniel Yuval, and he is ten years old. Here's the background . . ."

In early February 2010, Daniel and his family heard that snow was falling in the Golan Heights, a rare event, and on the afternoon of February 6, they drove two hours from their home in the suburbs of Tel Aviv, excited to witness their first snowfall. They had no way of knowing that throughout the region, snow had covered wooden signs painted with big red letters meant to warn hikers: "Danger—Landmines."

During the drive, Daniel talked with his father about landmines. His father, Guy, told him that mines had been left over from the past wars, and Daniel asked him a prophetic question: "What would be the chances of coming across one?" His father replied that the chances were very low.

Hundreds of cars had driven up to the Golan to enjoy the snow, and there was a long line snaking down the highway. The police told the Yuval family that, because of the heavy traffic, they should drive in a different direction than the mountain, so they stopped on the side of the road. Daniel's mother, Tali, stayed in the car with his two younger sisters, Rona and Gigi, who were cold and sleeping in their car seats. Daniel got out of the car with his father, his brother Yoav, and his sister Amit. They all raced to the top of the hill; Daniel got there first because he was the most competitive. He noticed a large stone covered with ice and glistening in the sun a few feet away. "Something told me I had to get to that rock, and I told my older sister to follow me," said Daniel.

His world exploded just a step away from that stone. Daniel lost consciousness and, with no idea what had happened, woke up on the other side of the rock. "I could hear my sister screaming—she was partially blinded—and I tried to stand up but felt an incredible pain and fell down," Daniel told me. His father ran to his side and told him that everything would be OK as he took off his shirt and bandaged his son's bloody leg. They realized that they had entered a minefield that had been placed there forty years earlier. Guy carried Daniel and Amit to an ambulance with hesitation and fear in every step.

Daniel told me that he had been painfully aware of everything around him, but still so confused and afraid. He kept saying to himself, "I am strong, I am brave," feeling that he needed to say this to stay alive.

An emergency helicopter arrived and flew the two children to a hospital. Guy, Tali, and their other children followed behind in their car, stuck in heavy traffic as the helicopter flew overhead. It was a mother's worst nightmare.

Daniel woke up from surgery at the hospital with his right leg missing below his knee, and he had lost most of the calf muscle on his left leg. The first thing he told his mother was, "I don't want this to happen to other children. Something needs to be done!" Daniel was mature beyond his years, and through his pain, he deeply believed that the public needed to be informed of the suffering caused by millions of landmines silently lurking in the ground around the world, waiting for innocent footsteps to take a wayward step.[8]

Jerry told me that after hearing about the story on Israeli television, he'd visited Daniel in the hospital, where the young boy had offered Jerry an objective, mature accounting of what had happened. "There was no self-pity in him," Jerry told me. "He looked up at me from his hospital bed and said six words: 'I want a world without landmines.'"

"I told him I knew someone who could help," Jerry said and then went silent, letting the implications sink in. As excited as I was about serving in the Holy Land, adding another country to the already over-burdened map of our tiny organization would be a high-stakes gamble.

"Israel is halfway around the world," I stammered, grasping at any lame excuse I could find. Every Roots of Peace operation was halfway around the world.

Jerry shrugged and said, "I promised Daniel I'd ask. It was worth a try." He knew I couldn't help but be lured by his offer.

"My dad just turned eighty," I said, "and we made plans to be together as a family this summer. It's been years since we took time off . . ." I was embarrassed listening to my own feeble excuses and knew in my heart that this was going to happen. My spiritual life was rooted in the Holy Land, and if there was a chance to help clear mines from the land of Jesus and Mary, how could I refuse? I thought that the price of such a privilege, however, would be once again disappointing my family by leaving. I'd never felt so comfortably uncomfortable in my life.

Jerry could have simply picked up the phone and called me, but he hadn't. He'd flown almost three thousand miles to tell me in person about

---

8 . Daniel's sister Amit eventually recovered from her blindness and went on to serve as a soldier for the Israeli army.

TOP: With Nancy and Frank Yih, former president of the Rotary Club of Shanghai, who donated one million Chinese RMB to turn mines to vines in Quảng Tri, Vietnam.

MIDDLE: In Vietnam in 2015. Photo courtesy of Frankie Frost.

BOTTOM: In Quảng Tri with Vietnamese mother who lost her son to a cluster bomb. Photo courtesy of Frankie Frost.

TOP: With a local resident among black pepper trees, which grow in a former Vietnam War battlefield.

ABOVE: Meeting with Monsignor Paul Phan and a Buddhist monk in Quảng Trị, Vietnam. Photo courtesy of Phan Tan Lam.

RIGHT: Shrapnel from unexploded ordnance in Vietnam. Photo courtesy of Frankie Frost.

TOP: A landmine survivor hands Heidi a cluster of chôm chôm, a fruit native to Vietnam, which was grown on a former minefield. Photo courtesy of Phan Tan Lam.

ABOVE: Planning to detonate unexploded ordnance in Vietnam. Photo courtesy of Frankie Frost.

TOP: Presenting Pope Francis with a white rose in 2018, a symbol of turning mines to vines. Photo courtesy of the Vatican.

ABOVE: Walking the streets of Husan village, located west of Bethlehem, with a Palestinian shepherd, who lost his right hand to a landmine, and an Israeli colonel.

RIGHT: With Cardinal Peter Turkson at the baptismal site of Jesus along the Israel-Jordan border, which is mined.

TOP: Meeting His Excellency Mahmoud Abbas, president of the State of Palestine and Palestinian National Authority, in Ramallah, West Bank.

ABOVE: Discussing the Minefield Clearance Act with Israeli Prime Minister Benjamin Netanyahu and Daniel Yuval at the Knesset in Jerusalem, Israel.

TOP: Then-president and CEO of the Skoll Foundation Sally Osberg, Sir Ben Kingsley, Robert Redford, and Jeffrey Skoll present the Skoll Award for Social Entrepreneurship to Heidi Kühn in Oxford, England, in 2006.

ABOVE: The author in a former battlefield located in the Shomali Plain of Afghanistan, just north of Kabul. This Afghan vineyard was demined thanks to funds from Diane Disney Miller. Today, fresh grapes flourish in what was once war-ravaged ground.

Daniel. In my life, I'd said no to a lot of people, but I'd never said no to Jerry and wasn't about to start now. He was way ahead of me.

"First," Jerry said, "we'll visit Bethlehem, then the Golan Heights, and right away we'll have to evaluate the situation on the ground and study details for making the Holy Land landmine-free." As far as he was concerned, we were already there. After he left, I recited a prayer, because this was one of those moments when thanks were in order, as well as an earnest request for help figuring out how to do it all—and how to let my family know.

Arriving home, I repeated Daniel's story for my husband and children and asked them how they'd feel if I accepted Jerry's invitation to bring Roots of Peace to Israel. Their support washed over me in an instant, and I knew I didn't need to worry. My family had become as committed as I was to the mission of Roots of Peace and had never been less than enthusiastic about opportunities to expand. This time was no exception.

Most people traveling to the Middle East confront a problem at customs—namely, suspicion caused by decades of conflict. If an American looking to enter Afghanistan has a passport stamped in Israel, that's going to be a hurdle to entry. And *Kabul* stamped in the passport of someone wanting to enter Tel Aviv will be just as big a hurdle. I wasn't in the US Foreign Service, which made me even more of a red flag at customs desks. Fortunately, the State Department had extended me the rare privilege of having two passports, and so in July 2010, sixteen hours after departing San Francisco, our plane touched down in Tel Aviv and the right passport got me through customs in short order.

There to greet us was our translator, Dhyan Or, whose fluency in Arabic, English, and Hebrew would prove immensely valuable in the weeks ahead. We drove to the YMCA Three Arches Hotel in Jerusalem, a historic hotel located across the street from the more modern King David Hotel, where international diplomats often stay. The Three Arches enjoys a unique reputation: It was built specifically as a place where followers of all three Abrahamic faiths could meet as equals. There is a plaque on the wall of the garden, leading to the bell tower, that reads, "Here is a place whose atmosphere is peace, where political and religious jealousies can be forgotten, and international unity fostered and developed." This was my first time to Israel, and the message was a welcome reassurance that I had arrived at my spiritual home.

The feeling of homecoming deepened the next morning when I woke to the sounds of church bells and calls to prayer echoing out from nearby mosques, mixing with cries of produce vendors in the streets below. To spiritually charge our first day in Jerusalem, Jerry and I drove to the Old City and took a brief walk down the Via Dolorosa, the processional route that Christians honor as the path Jesus was forced to take to his crucifixion.

Then we returned to the Three Arches, where the CEO, Forsan Hussein, had generously arranged for us to use the hotel's outdoor pagoda for our Roots of Peace meetings. The pagoda was lovely, but I shuddered as I looked more closely at the ceiling. It was riddled with bullet holes.

Our scheduling committee had organized meetings with several potential business partners on that warm summer morning. Our first guest, Dr. Avner Goren, was the most prominent archaeologist in the Holy Land. As soon as he arrived, I recognized him from his many interviews with Christiane Amanpour on CNN. Avner, who had lived for several years with Bedouins in the Sinai Desert, was a renowned authority on

Israel's archaeological history. His interest coincided with ours—namely, to find ways to demine sacred sites around Israel and Palestine. Also joining us was the head of the United Nations Mine Action Service and representatives from the Quartet on the Middle East, a group formed by the European Union, Russia, the United Nations, and the United States; Tony Blair, former prime minister of the United Kingdom, was at the time serving as the Quartet's special envoy.

We sat at a round table under the pagoda and discussed the most efficient way to secure the Israeli government's cooperation for our effort to eliminate the mines that had been planted during decades of armed conflict. The bill we would propose needed a name, and we settled on one that conveyed our intentions in no uncertain terms: the Minefield Clearance Act. Jerry had done his homework and knew all the right people to introduce me to, in support of a young boy's vision for a mine-free world.

Now, we needed to give the proposal weight. If the Knesset, Israel's legislative body, were going to approve the bill and possibly contribute to our effort, we would need a well-researched and well-written action plan. Where were the mines we proposed to defuse? How many were there? By what means were we proposing to find and neutralize them? What would it cost? How many people and what equipment would be needed? As familiar as our Roots of Peace staff was with these questions, answers varied according to location, and our guests were among the most qualified people in the country to help advise us how to customize our approach for Israel.

One guest in particular, Boris Krasny, proved critical to securing government approval. Boris's lobbying firm, Policy One, was renowned for its success at establishing relationships between clients and the Israeli government, and was expert at navigating the politically tricky waters of the Knesset.

Another participant, Tzachi Hanegbi, chairman of the Knesset Foreign Affairs and Defense Committee, spelled out in stark terms the extent of the crisis: Buried under the Holy Land were an estimated 1.5 million landmines and UXOs. The number elicited groans of shock. The members of the Roots of Peace contingent were familiar with such huge numbers from our work elsewhere in the world, but compared with Croatia or Afghanistan, the Holy Land was geographically minute; the sheer concentration of live mines in Israel was unprecedented.

The landmines laid during the 1950s and 1960s contaminate a combined area of 50,000 acres in the Golan Heights, in the Arava Valley, and along the Jordan River. This includes more than 300,000 landmines contaminating 5,000 acres of agricultural and residential land in the West Bank, with unexploded ordnance making even more sites inaccessible.

We added those devastating statistics to our proposal, which was beginning to spell out the economic as well as moral importance of demining: Apart from thousands of lives saved each year, the Minefield Clearance Act would transform condemned fields into profitable agricultural lands, which would generate funds for social welfare programs and increase tourism in the region.

Working with Hanegbi, we created maps that indicated which of the holy sites were most heavily mined, regardless of whose holy sites they were. Landmines do not discriminate, and know no religious boundaries. They kill innocent pilgrims and children of all faiths, colors, and creeds.

With copies of the finished proposal in hand, we rented a large bus and set off to bring key members of the Knesset and members of the Rotary Club of Jerusalem to the heavily mined banks of the Jordan River, specifically to Qasr al-Yahud, the site where Christians, Muslims, and Jews gathered together to pray in their respective languages.

"This is a powerful site," Avner told us. "It was here that Jesus was baptized by John, Elijah rose to heaven, the Israelites crossed over into Canaan, and Mohammad walked the path of Abraham."

Driving from Jerusalem, we passed the road to Jericho, where the Good Samaritan had reached out to help the poor on the side of the road two thousand years before. Today, the poorest of the poor tend to be the most exposed to the danger of landmines. I shook my head in shame, thinking of how little we had progressed in terms of compassion over the past two thousand years.

We entered Qasr al-Yahud and noticed hundreds of red signs warning, "Landmines." Barbed-wire fences separated the black paved road from stretches of desert on either side where thousands of landmines had been deployed during the wars of 1948 and 1967. None of them had yet been removed.

As we approached the river, there was a chained fence to our right, blocking the entrance to a Franciscan church where, I was told, the altar had been booby-trapped. Surrounding the church was a garden where a few dead trees were visible. Praising the land of Israel for its fruit trees is a tradition dating back to the Bible, which describes the shade of the grapevine and the fig tree as a metaphor for the idyllic peace we all await,[9] yet barren palm trees were all that remained of the church garden.

---

9. Deuteronomy 8:8.

The ten thousand or so pilgrims who flocked to this baptismal site of Jesus every January for the feast of St. John the Baptist were obliged to celebrate at a distance: The thick chain surrounding the entrance prevented anyone from entering.

"I needed you to see this for yourself," Jerry said. "The Christian world's third most holy site is a death zone."

"I had no idea," I said. "It's a violation of all that is holy."

Beyond the Franciscan church, there were other monasteries—Coptic, Ethiopian, Greek and Russian Orthodox, and Syrian—also surrounded by landmine-infested fields. Nearby was the Jordan River, where Jesus had been baptized by John.

"With global warming," Jerry said, "floods unearth the landmines on the edge of the riverbank. The mines float downstream to places where pilgrims assemble. What would Jesus say?"

To mark the occasion, Roots of Peace had purchased an olive tree. A church official opened the locked gate, and we carefully traversed a narrow strip of demined land. We planted the tree in the church's barren garden, and I knelt down and placed a basket containing barley, dates, figs, grapes, pomegranates, olives, and wheat—Judaism's Seven Species— next to it. Kneeling down next to me, Tzachi Hanegbi said, "The work of Roots of Peace transcends religion and politics." Together, we agreed to dedicate the Minefield Clearance Act to young Daniel Yuval, whose story had initiated our efforts in the Holy Land.

Daniel had understood the moment after the blast that his leg was gone. As a little boy, he was aware of the situation and mostly upset that he was not able to go to the judo tournament he had been training for, or to run as fast as before the injury.

Jerry introduced me to Daniel only five months after his tragic ordeal. As a mother of four children, it was painful for me to look into the eyes of this little boy and promise him a landmine-free world, yet I told him I would do everything in my power to make his dream a reality.

He told me with a sweet voice that his rehabilitation had been very difficult. He had to wake up every day at 5 A.M. and start painful physical therapy, yet he was extremely determined. Daniel was my inspiration as I commuted to the Holy Land more than a dozen times—going back and forth from Tel Aviv to Ramallah, over a wall. The political landmines meant nothing to me—all I could hear was the voice of a child crying out for a landmine-free world. Daniel gave me the courage to look forward and to continue believing in our mutual dream.

The Knesset's 120 members vote on all laws in Israel, elect the country's president and prime minister, approve its cabinet, and supervise the government's many programs. Proposals for new legislation such as ours are presented to the Knesset for members to vote on: yes or no. A proposal has a much better chance of approval if it is endorsed by the prime minister, and we had been given an exceptional opportunity to present our plan directly to Prime Minister Benjamin Netanyahu. However, first, we had to meet with the distinguished members of the Knesset.

On February 6, 2012, the one year anniversary of Daniel's tragic landmine accident, we drove directly to the Knesset. As our van arrived in West Jerusalem, we gazed up at the Knesset's magnificent modern white structure perched on a hilltop. On our approach to the security checkpoint, our six-foot-four Palestinian driver, Ismael, slouched down in his seat to make himself appear less threatening. He kept his head lowered as well. He was a proud man, and sometimes the resentment in his heart over Palestine's troubled history showed as a silent grimace on his face.

Israeli police armed with machine guns checked our papers and waved us through, and Ismael waited in the car while young Daniel and I walked up the steps to the entrance. The police ushered us into a reception room and asked that we surrender our bags for inspection. Cameras installed in the four corners of the room tracked our every move. Our bags were approved, and the security people escorted us down long a corridor. I held Daniel's hand. He had done a fine job of learning to walk with a prosthetic leg.

"What you're doing takes courage," I told him as we walked. "You're about to ask the Israeli government to sign legislation that will ban landmines. I'm very proud of you."

"I don't want other kids to go through what I've gone through," he said, bowing his head.

We met with Deputy Minister of Defense Matan Vilnai, and the meeting went well. A few weeks later, on March 14, 2011, the Israeli Knesset unanimously (43-0) approved the Minefield Clearance Act, which marked Israel's first effort to address the landmine contamination at a national level, and limited demining to areas deemed "not essential to national security." While I was not present in the room at the time, the act's passage took place one year after the landmine detonation Daniel had suffered. This brave little boy's story resulted in our campaign, which made headlines across Israel and beyond. We, a mother and child, along with Jerry White, were widely credited for the legislation's ultimate success.

The legislation created hundreds of jobs for demining workers, both Israeli and Palestinian, and led to creation of the Israeli National Mine

Action Authority (INMAA) through the Ministry of Defense, with a budget of over $27 million. The legislation also led to formation of the Palestinian Mine Action Center, based in Ramallah. With the legal and managerial foundation in place, Roots of Peace was ready to begin its work in the Holy Land.

A few months later, when Matan Vilnai, Israel's minister of defense, visited our family home in San Rafael for a private dinner, he confided to our other guests, "Frankly, we passed the legislation because we were afraid to say no to Heidi." Those who knew me burst out laughing. I couldn't blame them.

Over the years, I developed a strong bond of friendship with the Yuval family, and on the occasion of Daniel's thirteenth birthday, he invited me to attend his bar mitzvah. I was the only Christian among hundreds of guests attending this sacred ceremony in the city of Ramat HaSharon. Daniel whispered in my ear, "Auntie Heidi, I don't even mind if you wear your blue-and-gold cross around your neck into the temple. You are a mother to all children who suffer from landmines." I glanced down, taken by the kindness in his young words, only to see the cross given to me on Christmas Eve in Bethlehem. It was not meant to be a statement. I had worn this cross among the Muslims in Afghanistan and the Communists in Vietnam—never to offend, but only as a sign of protection and of gratitude after overcoming the landmine of cancer in my life. As the ceremony began, as was customary, Daniel recited verses from the Torah he'd memorized. And though he spoke only in Hebrew, I felt a swelling of pride in my heart. Holding the hand of his mother, Tali, surrounded by her other children seated in the front row, I was very proud to be Daniel's American "mother."

Later in the evening, there was a large celebration with family and friends at a chic club. In the video shown to hundreds of guests, they'd included various clips of our journey to help bring forth the historic Minefield Clearance Act. It was a deeply touching moment.

That evening, we returned to Daniel's home, and he insisted on giving me his bedroom as his family's guest; he slept on the living room couch. As I nestled into his twin bed against the wall, I gazed at a poster of him surfing in the Mediterranean Sea only three years earlier with two healthy and strong limbs, toes firmly clenched to the board. As I closed my eyes, I imagined what a young boy can dream of once he's lost a leg to a landmine.

The next day, Daniel invited me to join him for a special meeting with Netanyahu. Together, as photographers clicked away, we entered a large room filled with reporters and a crowd that had assembled to watch. Daniel's mother, Tali, was present with Daniel's sister Amit and his younger brother, Yoav. Members of the Knesset stepped forward to commend Daniel for his bravery and for his role in the historic legislation about to be discussed.

As Netanyahu entered the room, surrounded by armed guards, an assistant pointed us out and whispered something into his ear in Hebrew. My guess was that he was explaining Roots of Peace and our track record in other parts of the world. The assistant then pointed to young Daniel and seemed to be recounting his tragic history. The prime minister walked up to Daniel and shook his hand.

"Is there something you wish to tell me?" Netanyahu said.

Daniel looked up at the prime minister and, in a soft voice, replied, "Thank you for approving the [Minefield Clearance Act.] Please tell the Knesset that this is the best thing they can do for the Holy Land." Then

Daniel pointed to me and said, "This is Heidi Kühn. She is the founder of Roots of Peace and helps children around the world who suffer from landmines. She's been like a second mother to me after my accident in the minefield."

The prime minister shook my hand and nodded. He had children of his own, and his expression said he understood the importance of this legislation.

I pointed to Tali and said, "No mother should have to see what that woman saw: her child losing his limbs. Tali Yuval has four other children at home, and she's raised them with great courage."

Netanyahu looked thoughtful for a moment, then said, "I would like you and Daniel and your associates to come with me. I want to show you the Plenum Hall. This is where the Knesset votes on historic proposals, including yours."

With the prime minister leading the way, we walked down the stairs together. To my embarrassment, one of my shoes caught on the hem of my floor-length, black velvet coat and slipped off my foot. Netanyahu noticed, bent down, and retrieved my shoe.

"Madam," he said, "I believe you have lost your slipper." Then he extended his hand, returning my shoe with a slight bow. The reference to a similar scene in the Disney movie *Cinderella* was obvious to everyone.

"Mr. Prime Minister, you are a true prince," I said. Around us, the press was having a field day, snapping photos and stumbling over themselves to get a shot of Prince Netanyahu and the magic slipper. Daniel thought it was hysterical.

"Only you, Auntie Heidi," he said, laughing. "Nobody else would this happen to."

"There is a saying in America," I replied. "When life hands you lemons, make lemonade."

During that initial visit to the Holy Land, before we met with the Knesset, Jerry took me through a series of armed checkpoints along Israel's barrier wall. Built in the West Bank during the Second Intifada, which began in September 2000, it was justified by the Israeli government as necessary to keep terrorists out—a way to stop the wave of violence triggered by the uprising. Palestinians call it a racial-segregation or apartheid wall. It may have been effective in its own way, but it was causing hardships for everyone and served as a scar on the Holy Land.

Question as I might the necessity for such a dividing wall, I could not risk taking a public stance on it. If Roots of Peace was going to be effective in removing landmines in the Holy Land, we needed to maintain our status as a neutral, nonpolitical organization working solely in the interest of peace. Since our avowed reason for being there was to alleviate the pain and suffering felt by both Israeli and Palestinian children in fields poisoned by landmines, I had to remain silent, not out of acquiescence but of necessity, especially when we ventured north to Bethlehem.

It was a hot day in July 2010 when I first set foot in Bethlehem and realized that I was walking in the footsteps of blessed Mother Mary. After meandering through the ancient lanes of the biblical village, I entered St. Catherine's Church at Manger Square, where I witnessed my first Arab Catholic Mass. Around me were Palestinians at prayer. I joined them and dropped into a dreamlike state. In my mind's eye, I could see tears from heaven streaming down like rain, as Mary cried for her children who had lost their way from the Garden of Eden and had planted mines that could destroy any living being who took a wayward step. When I came out of my reverie, I saw rain falling outside the church windows, a rare event in that part of the world.

We walked up Star Road, the path traced by Mary as she rode on a donkey led by her husband, Joseph, to the inn, hoping for shelter. On the top of the hill, a beautiful Palestinian mother of four, Fadwa Abu Laban, opened the door of her home to welcome us. Fadwa, an advocate of landmine removal in the area, had been introduced to me by Jerry White. As we entered, the aroma of freshly baked chocolate cake was intoxicating. We sat down and spoke for hours about the long, arduous task of removing landmines, and she agreed to form a partnership. Together, we two mothers, one American, the other Palestinian, held hands and vowed to do what we could to end the scourge. Fadwa became a dear friend and supporter in the historic demining of the fields of Bethlehem.

I spent the Fourth of July with Fadwa that year. We brought a group of girls to the Three Arches YMCA, and I had the honor of teaching them to swim for the first time in their lives. They were covered from head to toe, as is customary in Muslim culture—no bikinis, like in California! I brought several watermelons to honor the Fourth of July holiday as it was transpiring in America. The laughter and splashing at the YMCA that day sounded like hope in this suffering region, and it made me smile as I thought of my own children back home.

Next, we drove to Husan, a Muslim village only four miles from the site of the manger where Jesus was born. There, we were greeted by Omar, an elderly shepherd dressed in traditional white robes and wearing a red checkered headband. He extended his right arm in greeting, and as I reached out, I was surprised to find a metal hook at the end of it. He told us his story.

As a boy, Omar played in the fields around his home and tended sheep with his grandfather near the site where the biblical battle between David and Goliath was reputed to have occurred. In 1948, war broke out, and Jordanian soldiers planted landmines in the fields surrounding Omar's home. Omar and his childhood friends were warned by their parents to stay out of these dangerous fields, but one day, he heard a loud blast and the scream of a man from the forbidden area. Setting aside his own safety, Omar rushed into the field to help the man.

Boom!

Omar's right arm was blown off, but Omar and the wounded man managed to help each other out of the field and to a road, where they were picked up and taken to the local hospital.

Sixty-two years later, Omar was a grandfather standing next to me on the side of that same field where his life had changed forever, offering to help us remove the mines from his beloved homeland.

"I've lost eight childhood friends to landmines in this field," he said. "They were just children, playing like all children do."

At that moment, Omar's grandchildren called to him, and he waved his metal hook to greet them. It was the kind of simple gesture that can reinforce a person's dedication to do whatever it takes, for however long it takes, to ensure that not one child more dies from a landmine. Shepherds in the fields of Bethlehem should not wave metal hooks from a landmine blast.

Before all our efforts with the Knesset, in November 2010, young Daniel Yuval and his family flew to Washington, DC, to join Jerry

White and me for a series of meetings and presentations at the State Department. We spoke with Senator John McCain, and Daniel's heartfelt story clearly moved the senior statesman. Tim Reiser from Senator Patrick Leahy's office greeted us as we went to the Stimson Center, a nonpartisan think tank, for a panel discussion led by Ambassador Lincoln Bloomfield. Then we met with Israel's consul general, Ido Aharoni, who organized a reception at which I presented both Daniel and Jerry with Roots of Peace Global Citizen awards.

Next, we traveled via train from Washington, DC, to New York City. I recall that we were a bit late in catching the train, and young Daniel was obliged to run fast with his prosthetic leg. He limped in great pain but refused to slow down. In New York, we arranged meetings for Daniel at the United Nations and with Jerry White's cousin, Erin Burnett, an CNBC News anchor who invited us to join him on the set. The interview aired nationally.

Meanwhile, Gary and I continued to manage our programs in both Afghanistan and Vietnam while raising our own children in California. It was a delicate balancing act. Early in 2010, Gary and I had submitted a proposal for $30 million to Karl Eikenberry, US ambassador to Afghanistan, for a program we called the Commercial Horticulture and Agricultural Marketing Program (CHAMP). The proposal was approved, and as a consequence, that year was one of constant travel back and forth, monitoring Roots of Peace initiatives in both the Middle East and Central Asia. By this time, Roots of Peace was now successfully implementing our mines-to-vines model—demining and replanting—in Afghanistan, Bosnia-Herzegovina, Cambodia, Croatia, Iraq, Israel/Palestine, and Vietnam. And all this was happening while I raised four wonderful children on our home front in San Rafael.

By then, all of us working to transform mines to vines had learned that trying to do good in the world requires much personal sacrifice—often more than we think we are capable of. What empowers some people, I've often wondered, to achieve more than they think themselves capable of achieving? I choose to believe that once we commit wholeheartedly to a noble cause, there are higher forces that steer us in a certain direction and that come to our aid when we are in need. I've learned that when you are really, truly doing good work, things come—miracles, coincidences, help, wisdom—that are meant to tell you, "See? Keep going. You're on the right path."

One such moment occurred for me when, without any prior notice, an invitation arrived from the Vatican. It had been one of my life's most memorable events when, some years before, I had been blessed to have an audience with Pope Benedict XVI. But many people meet the pope, and I hadn't expected him to remember me. Then this invitation arrived in February 2011, inviting me to give a speech on *Mater et Magistra*, the mystery of the Mother and the Teacher, before an audience in the Vatican. For someone like me, motivated by deep faith, honors don't get much greater than that.

Obviously, the credit for such an honor goes to many, many people. Roots of Peace is a big team, and all of us do our best for this noble cause of demining and resuscitating farmlands. Still, an invitation from the Vatican to a housewife turned activist who started out in her basement was a good reminder that the sky is the limit if your cause is just and your determination strong.

And just as fast, fortunes can be reversed. A few weeks later, on April 20, 2011, I was rushed to the Kaiser Permanente San Rafael Medical

Center for an emergency hysterectomy. The surgery did not go well. Gary was in Afghanistan, so my father and my oldest son, Brooks, signed the papers to assume responsibility in case of my death. After eight hours under the knife, I was diagnosed with a life-threatening infection contracted during surgery. Our Catholic priest arrived and administered the sacrament called Anointing of the Sick. Cheryl Jennings and her husband, Rick Pettibone, visited me each evening after her job as anchor of the ABC7 News broadcast, dressed in blue hospital scrubs and masks.

I told the doctors and nurses I was scheduled to speak at the Vatican a few weeks later and that they had to help me get out of there. They looked at me as though I was overmedicated and clearly hallucinating.

"I'm sorry, Mrs. Kühn," the head of the medical team said. "It's impossible for you to fly. You could die at 30,000 feet after such an operation."

"Doctor," I told him, "if I die 30,000 feet in the air, I'll be that much closer to God. Now, find me some paper so I can write my speech. You do the medical work, and I'll do the spiritual work."

The nurses gathered at my door and watched me write. I overheard them whisper in disbelief, "Poor dear—she thinks she's going to give a speech at the Vatican and have an audience with the pope."

I thought of them fondly as I boarded the plane for Rome a few weeks later. I was walking in faith, not fear. I can still remember today how painful it was climbing the stairs of the Vatican with Gary by my side. Thanks to God, I forgot about the pain by the time I was asked to stand and deliver my speech.

Monsignor Labib Kobti of St. Thomas More Church, referred to as *Abouna* (Arabic for "father"), came into my life on August 31,

2011, the anniversary of the death of Princess Diana of Wales. That day happened to be the monsignor's birthday, and George Wesolek, director of public policy and social concerns at the Archdiocese of San Francisco, suggested it would be a good occasion for us to meet. George had told Abouna of my deep faith in the Blessed Mother and of my vision to turn mines to vines worldwide, and though Abouna was skeptical, he took the meeting as a matter of courtesy. Born in Lebanon, he had worked for years in both Bethlehem and Rome and spoke many languages. He knew the ways of the church, and we quickly warmed to each other and formed a strong friendship "in the name of Mary," as he put it.

A few weeks later, I was invited by the International Women's Forum (IWF) to attend the tenth anniversary commemoration to the 9/11 attacks led by General Barbara Faulkenberry in Germany. As we stood on the bluffs of the Rhine River, the incision from my recent hysterectomy burst open, and blood was oozing from my stomach. We were scheduled to meet Chancellor Angela Merkel, but instead, Nannette Griswold escorted me into an ambulance and I was taken by emergency to the Berlin Hospital. It was a surreal moment, with sirens blasting on September 11, 2011, as this stigmata continued to bleed. I was stabilized and immediately flown home, where the doctors at Kaiser Hospital performed surgery again. It was a bit of a miracle that I survived the strenuous train ride and flight home.

Monsignor Kobti witnessed all this suffering and invited me to attend the Nativity Mass on Christmas Eve in Bethlehem—a rare honor bestowed to few in the world. I was determined to go as a way of putting behind me the brush with death I'd had four months before. The monsignor extended his invitation to my husband and children as well, but when we discussed the idea later, they all admitted to me that they'd rather spend Christmas together at home. I was a bit disappointed, but who could blame them? For so long, they'd traveled constantly on behalf of Roots of Peace. We came to a compromise: I'd help with the family's Christmas preparations, then leave for Bethlehem on my own. Together, we decorated the house and enjoyed an early Christmas dinner complete with all the trimmings, and then I packed my bags. I was determined to leave a legacy that the real home of Christmas was not in the shopping mall; it was in the heart of Bethlehem.

Shortly before leaving, I mentioned the upcoming journey to the Holy Land to two of my best friends, Mary and Joseph Cresalia. This was the same couple who had hiked Mount Tamalpais with me when I first had the vision of turning mines to vines. Mary and Joseph had nine children, yet the minute they learned about the trip, they insisted that I couldn't possibly go alone, not so soon after surgery.

"We're going with you," Mary told me matter-of-factly.

That's how I ended up checking into the inn in Bethlehem on Christmas Eve with Mary and Joseph. The innkeeper shook his head in disbelief and said, "Merry Christmas!"

On January 1, 2012, my husband and my youngest son, Christian, decided they didn't want to miss out on New Year's with me and joined me in Jerusalem. We had been invited by the Latin Patriarch of Jerusalem, Fouad Twal, for the World Day of Peace, and Christian, age sixteen, the only one of my children yet to join us on a mission, was invited to be the youth speaker at this internationally televised Mass at the Church of the Holy Sepulchre—truly a great honor. Two generous Roots of Peace donors, Paul and Shirley Dean, owners of Spiriterra Vineyards in Napa Valley, also joined us for this occasion and made a generous donation of $100,000 for removal of landmines in Husan, that Muslim village just four miles from where Jesus was born. It was a time of great celebration, after which we met with leaders of both the Muslim and the Jewish communities for further good cheer. We ended the day at the home of Israeli archaeologist Avner Goren on the bluffs of Mount Olive as we watched the first sunset of the New Year.

Together, we celebrated my birthday in Bethlehem, and a large candle the size of a firecracker was placed in my cake by the Palestinians. It was presented in a dark corner of the room. As the fire was lit, there was a gasp by Paul and Shirley and a couple of others, who thought it might be a terrorist attack. Yet it was only a flame lighting a torch—representing my fifty-four birthday candles!

The groundwork required to start the program in the country occupied my month as I traveled back and forth, earning trust in both Jerusalem and Ramallah. A firm foundation of trust among both Israelis and Palestinians was essential to the success of the program, and I was determined to make this work for a higher purpose. Days blended into weeks.

My flight home departed in late January. Later, I glanced at the calendar and discovered that on this trip, I had stayed forty days and forty nights.

The following year was absorbed with filling out the reams of paperwork necessary to obtain permission for Roots of Peace to remove landmines in the fields surrounding Bethlehem. It took twelve flights from California for meetings in both Jerusalem and Ramallah, a ritual of shuttle diplomacy known as going "over the wall" or "over the fence."

In January 2013, ABC7 News anchor Cheryl Jennings and her husband, Rick Pettibone, flew with me to Tel Aviv to cover the Roots of

Peace story for San Francisco Bay Area television viewers. We made three stops: First, we visited Daniel Yuval's home and watched him, outfitted with a prosthetic leg, play soccer with other boys. Next, we visited Latin patriarch Fouad Twal, who presented me with the Catholic Church's first peace medal. Finally, we traveled "over the wall" to Ramallah and the headquarters of the Palestinian Liberation Organization to speak with Palestinian leaders about the importance of our work in the region. Cheryl's report on that extraordinary encounter earned her an award for excellence in journalism.

By May 2013, all paperwork had been approved, all permits secured, all contracts signed, and all funding in place, and we were finally ready to begin demining in the Holy Land. That was the moment when Israeli and Arab workers realized that agreeing to work for Roots of Peace meant agreeing to work side by side with their "enemy." The feelings ran quite deep. One Israeli worker, for instance, told me that when he signed on for this assignment in the West Bank, his wife cried and kissed him goodbye, fearing the worst from the Palestinian truck drivers. Israelis had never gone into Palestine to remove landmines, only to plant them, and their families were concerned that their brave husbands and fathers would not come home.

Teams of Arab and Israeli workers were already at a standoff when we arrived with our staff of experts. From the moment we showed up, it was clear that tensions were running high. Rick Pettibone had returned to the Holy Land with me; we arrived through the back door of Amman, Jordan, and crossed the dangerous river over the King Hussein Bridge into Palestine. There were six checkpoints as we carried our luggage past armed guards in hot temperatures. Neither team of contracted workers had ever worked so closely with the "enemy" before, and it was clear that a decisive action was needed. I stepped forward and announced to both teams that either they immediately cease their suspicions and begin the work, or else Roots of Peace would withdraw its financial support. Nobody moved.

Omar, the elderly shepherd landmine survivor I had befriended in the Muslim village of Husan, stood nearby. I grabbed his good arm with one hand and, with the other, I grabbed Pini J. Dagan, owner of the Israeli demining company Quadro, and dragged them up the hillside to the edge of the field where eight children had died during the past six decades of war.

"Be careful! There are snipers on the other side of that hill! You could get shot!" yelled out one of the Palestinian truck drivers.

"Let them shoot a mother of four if they want!" I yelled back.

A crowd followed us up the hill, including an imam from a nearby mosque, rabbis and priests from surrounding villages, and merchants, all curious to see what would happen. We reached the top of the hill, and I began to pray. What choice did they have? The imam began to pray, the Catholic priest began to pray, the rabbis prayed, then the villagers began to pray. No one in that part of the world had ever attended such an interfaith service before. It was a rare display of unity noted even by local merchants, who handed out cups of ice to one and all. The Israeli deminers accepted the gifts and were a bit stunned by this gesture from their "enemies" on this hot day.

As the deminers returned to work, they heard gunshots from a distance and ducked for cover. The Palestinian tractor drivers laughed and reassured them. "Relax," they said. "On happy occasions, we shoot guns into the air. It's a tradition."

Tradition—there's a concept everybody could understand.

The mood grew lighter, friendlier, and at last Pini and Mati, owners of the Israeli demining company, felt confident enough to send their crews into the minefields, entrusting their employees' lives to the Palestinians.

Once the demining was completed for the day, a young Palestinian man rode his horse across the cleared land, galloping across the fields of Bethlehem with his head held high, chanting "Glory be to God! And peace to his people on Earth!"

Peace and goodwill really can unify us all. It was a moment that none of us would forget.

Fadwa Abu Laban, a Palestinian mother of four, was the Roots of Peace country director for the region. When her husband, Saleh, was a boy, he had been imprisoned for fifteen years by Israeli authorities for the "crime" of throwing rocks to protect himself against aggression. Saleh helped me greatly, and thanks in large part to his example of forgiveness, we earned the trust of both the mayor of Bethlehem and the imam of Bethlehem.

Saleh introduced me to the grand mufti of Jerusalem, the distinguished Muslim religious leader who performed weekly sermons from the steeple of the Dome of the Rock. It was the first time that a woman, American or otherwise, had been allowed into his offices in Ramallah. He listened to Saleh describe our work, then walked to his desk, picked up his holy wooden beads on which he had prayed five times a day for many years, and gently placed them in my hands.

"You are doing God's work for the sake of the children," he said. "Please accept these and pray for me."

Saleh and Fadwa could not believe their eyes. Not only had the grand mufti given me his personal prayers beads, but he'd also taken my hand, a woman's hand, something forbidden in Muslim culture.

"True Muslims do not bomb or kill," he said with a note of sadness in his voice. "These are not the teachings of Mohammad, and I am sorry when his teachings are betrayed. The true Muslim world is praying that you continue your noble work."

One amazing moment such as that can compensate for a lot of setbacks. It's been so important for me, whether or not I'm doing the kind of work that deals with children being blown up, that I cherish these profound moments when they occur, not take them for granted, and keep them like buried treasure in my soul for all time.

Every morning in Jerusalem, I followed a similar routine, walking at 6:30 A.M. from the Three Arches YMCA across the road, past the King David Hotel, and through the Jaffa Gate. I said good morning to the street vendors as they opened their shops for tourists, and they smiled back and waved. I arrived at the Holy Sepulchre, sank to my knees for Mass on the cold stone at 7 A.M., and meditated on the statue of Mary. The sculptor had chosen to depict her with a sword piercing her heart, epitomizing the pain she must have felt as she took her beloved son off the Cross. On the ceiling were carvings of grapevines and doves, the images I'd selected a decade before as the Roots of Peace logo. While in Bethlehem, on the other side of the fence, I would walk to the manger where Mary had nursed baby Jesus, which was in the shape of a star and set deep inside the church. It was impossible to avoid comparing the sacred shadows of the church with the deadly darkness of the landmines lying only a short distance away. Each morning, the priest ended his sermon with the words "Peace be with you. Go forth in peace to love and serve the world." I'd then sit quietly for hours until William, the security guard, began ushering in pilgrims and tourists.

One day, my disappointment over the lack of faster progress in the Holy Land must have shown on my face. Ismael, our driver, looked at me with a touch of pity and said, "Mrs. Kühn, every time you come to the Holy Land, you have me drive you to a minefield. Today, you will see the brighter side of life here in my country."

With that, we set out for the Sea of Galilee, Capernaum, Canaan, and Nazareth, and at each of these scenic stops, I got out of the van and prayed at the local church for guidance. We drove to Ein Kerem, a picturesque valley where there was a magnificent blue-tiled church that looked familiar, even though I had never been there before. Ismael showed me a brochure that revealed this was the Church of St. John the Baptist. Here, the Blessed Mother Mary had traveled two thousand years ago to visit her favorite cousin, Elizabeth. Still only a teenager, Mary was excited to tell her cousin about her pregnancy, and she traveled in haste. Elizabeth could not have children, but on the day she married Zechariah, an elderly priest, the archangel Gabriel appeared and blessed her. Elizabeth became pregnant with John, the cousin of Jesus, through whom the ancient rite of baptism connects Jesus with all of humanity.

Two thousand years later, landmines desecrated the ground surrounding this sacred baptismal site of Jesus, Qasr al-Yahud, where he had the realization that he was the son of God. While in Jerusalem, I would visit the Holy Sepulchre for Mass every morning, and, while in Bethlehem, I would visit the manger for Mass daily as well.

In October 2013, Cardinal Peter Turkson, president of the Pontifical Council for Justice and Peace, invited me to the Vatican to attend the fiftieth anniversary of the encyclical of *Pacem in terris* (Peace on Earth). When I spoke with him about the urgency of addressing landmines in the Holy Land, I learned that he wasn't aware of the landmine crisis, and the conversation led to an audience with Pope Francis along with my daughter, Kyleigh. At the audience, I presented His Holiness with a magnum of Grgich Hills Estate wine that Mike Grgich had autographed as a symbol of turning mines to vines. Then I described how it took only eight pounds to detonate a landmine, the average weight of a newborn child. Pope Francis took my daughter Kyleigh's hand, smiled, and said in a soft voice, "May God bless your holy work. Please pray for me."

It was not lost on me how many of the religious leaders I'd had the honor of meeting shared this trait of humility and asked for common people like me to pray for them.

The next week, after returning to California, a call came from Rome informing us that Cardinal Turkson would join me in the Holy Land to study the landmine situation. I shared this news with the other priests, but no one believed that a high-level official from the Vatican would join a mother in the Holy Land. And so, I traveled alone.

On November 1, 2013, All Saints' Day, Cardinal Turkson met me in Jerusalem with our trusted driver, Ismael, and together we visited minefields on sacred sites to study the crisis firsthand. First we walked the baptismal site of Jesus and the fields of Bethlehem. Then, at the Franciscan church where a chain-link fence prevented pilgrims from entering a minefield, we prayed for the resources, personal and otherwise, to eradicate mines from one of the holiest places on Earth.

As a little boy had once told me, "My name is Daniel—which in Hebrew means 'God is my judge'—and I accept that. This is my new life, without questioning. I remember the story of Daniel the prophet, who was saved from the den, and I know I am in the lion's den and I have to do good deeds to save myself. I have set new goals for the purpose of a landmine-free world."

Nearly a decade later, Daniel, now serving in the Israeli army, standing on one good leg, proudly stated, "We never know how strong we are until we are faced with disaster. Reaching that lone rock on the snowy day in the Golan changed my life forever. We all have our own 'rocks' that we are trying to reach. Some of them will empower us, and others will harm us. No matter what you face, you can always find the courage within you to rise up and enjoy the snowflakes."

CHAPTER ELEVEN

THE GAUNTLET

Overcoming the Taliban Attack

It is God who arms me with strength and keeps my way secure.

—PSALMS 18:32

E ven the most sincere prayers can't stave off all the evils of the world, as we discovered on March 28, 2014. On that day, a Taliban suicide bomber drove his car through the gates of the Christian day care center located next to the Roots of Peace house in Kabul and detonated his bomb. The explosion was heard throughout the city. Following behind in a car, five Taliban attackers stormed the center. At that same moment, they detonated a smaller bomb that blew open the gates of our Roots of Peace house, which was used as residential quarters for our expatri-ate staff. Two Afghan civilians died in the attack, one of them a young woman named Hanifa, age twenty-five, a fifth-year medical student who had volunteered for the first democratic election in Afghanistan. Another victim was Mustafa, age thirty, father of three, who had just lost his wife in childbirth and was the sole breadwinner for his family. In an instant, their dreams were blown away forever.

Luckily, our employees had taken the precaution of blocking the front gate to our property with an armored car. When the Taliban attackers stormed the property, the Roots of Peace staff retreated into the house. These were the same bedrooms where Gary and I had stayed only the month before.

After the initial explosion that destroyed the main gate, two of the expat staff were able to run to the roof, while three remained in their bedrooms.

When the Taliban made their way into the compound, the first grenades were detonated in the basement and in Rod's bedroom; his room was basically next to the entrance door. The next one exploded in Faustino's room. Both men, and another staff member, had planned to eat dinner at the compound that night but had received an invitation to dine with a friend instead. If they hadn't changed their plans at the last minute, Rod and Faustino would most likely be dead. To me, a miracle saved both of them.

One of our staff, Dustin, was entrenched in the second floor with Akbar, the Afghan security guard who was the real hero of the day. Akbar managed to shoot two Taliban terrorists as they were trying to reach the second floor. Both died on the stairway. If the terrorists had gotten to the second floor, everyone likely would have been killed. Dustin's laptop had a bullet hole right in the middle of it.

Another staff member, Hazman, hid under his bed, and every time a grenade shook the place, he jumped and hit the bottom of his bed. He stayed there during the entire attack, until Afghan security forces took control of the situation.

In the meantime, another of our staff, an Australian, ran to the roof wearing only his underwear and jumped from the four-story building into a tree on the street that cushioned his fall. Once he reached the ground, all scratched and in pain, an Afghan soldier immediately took him to a safe place and kindly gave him his jacket. To this day, he wears that jacket.

After the assault, the compound was heavily damaged, though not destroyed. Later, it turned out that the attackers had mistakenly thought the Roots of Peace staff were part of the Christian-run day care center, where they suspected the staff of converting Muslims to Christianity. The lives of twenty-five kindergarten children were spared that day.

After a few days in the Kabul Serena Hotel, all the expat staff members were moved to the Q Kabul Hotel, but after multiple attacks, and rumors that the Taliban was planning to assault several more places in Kabul, they were all evacuated to Dubai, where they stayed for about a week.

Even though Mohammad Sharif Osmani and his family were targeted by the Taliban, Sharif was courageous and kind enough to accompany them to the Kabul airport and make sure they boarded their plane without any further surprises.

While our family watched and listened to the attack—a grueling four and a half hours of panic and confusion—on Skype from the safety of our California home, the *New York Times* and the *Washington Post* called us for comments. Three of our four children were home and listened to the live attack with Gary and me, not knowing from moment to moment the status of our brave Roots of Peace staff trapped inside the compound.

Miraculously, no one among them was killed, as our Afghan guards bravely fought against the Taliban to protect the lives of Americans during a long, fierce gun battle. News traveled rapidly around the world, and US Army general John F. Campbell, commander of NATO's International Security Assistance Force, called to offer his support. The grand mufti from the Dome of the Rock in Jerusalem phoned me to say that the entire Muslim world was praying for us and that he was going to include us in his Friday prayers.

US Air Force general Barbara Faulkenberry was there for me again after the Taliban attack, pulling strings to get our Roots of Peace country director, Mohammad Sharif Osmani, his wife, Fawzia, and their three children safely out of Afghanistan and flown to Fairfax, California, near us. When the Taliban found out that Roots of Peace was led by a female CEO, the organization placed me at the top of its Facebook page with a target symbol superimposed on my face. Roots of Peace was featured in the centerfold of *Time* magazine with photos of the damaged compound.

After the attack, the only item in the Kabul office that remained intact amid the rubble was a wooden heart decorated with dried red roses, a Valentine's Day gift we had received from Afghan well-wishers of Roots of Peace. After the battle, soldiers and staff retrieved the carved red heart and sent it to us as a symbol of their untrammeled faith, hope, and love. Today, the heart of red roses that survived the Taliban attack hangs in the living room of our home as a symbol of the courage needed to bring peace in this world. For me, the carving represents the Sacred Heart of Jesus, a symbol expressing that, however much death is caused by hate, love is still the most powerful force in the world.

Still, the attack left me shaken. That evening, wanting to distract me, Gary took me to dinner at the Pelican Inn at Muir Beach. My gaze landed on words etched above the restaurant's fireplace: "Fear knocked at the door. Faith answered. No one was there."

The Taliban attack took place nearly sixteen years after the official launch of Roots of Peace. In that time, we had grown from one project in Croatia to almost a dozen on three continents. And yet we have barely scratched the surface: The work still to be done is enormous. More than sixty million landmines remain live in sixty countries, waiting to maim or kill innocent people living in war zones around the world.

On October 11, 2014, Barbara and Charlie Goodman, founders of the social action group Shifting Gears, organized a fundraiser at Checkers in Marin County to benefit the work of Roots of Peace in Quảng Tri Province. Barbara was a Pan Am stewardess during the Vietnam War and vividly remembered flying our troops back to Saigon after their leave.

More than 200 guests assembled to hear remarks about our progress in turning mines to vines. My son Tucker was emcee for the event. We flew in Huynh, the young man whose face had been so tragically disfigured by a landmine outside his home in Vietnam. Huynh, looking handsome in his first tuxedo, told his story to the distinguished audience, and his heart-rending narration helped raise over $125,000 that evening, a sum later matched by the State Department's PM/WRA.

As our fundraiser was taking place, back in Vietnam, a seventeen-year-old boy named Huan Van Tranh was fixing his bicycle on the side of the road. He could not afford a new bike and was constantly obliged to adjust the wheels on his old one. He picked up what he thought was a rock and began to pound it against a bent wheel, just as he had done many times before. The rock was a cluster munition. It exploded, blowing off his face and left arm. His mother came running to his side and with help from friends managed to lift him up and take him to a nearby hospital.

A month after the horrific incident, in November 2014, I visited young Huan in what may have been the most unsanitary hospital I'd ever seen, and certainly the saddest, with cries of pain issuing from every room. I approached Huan in his bed, and he grasped my arm with his remaining hand. We were quiet for a few minutes. I remember shaking with sadness when I saw how severely he had been burned. His mother noticed and wrapped her arm over my shoulder: two mothers grieving over the unbearable toll of war.

After a few minutes of gentle discussion, I presented Huan with a Roots of Peace bracelet to wear on his wrist. Noticing my discomfort, he lifted the stump of his arm as though saluting a thank you. It was such a tender gesture. I explained through my interpreter that the message on the bracelet was "Dig deeper," referring both to the act of digging out mines and also going deep spiritually and psychologically to maintain the commitment to doing so. But what could I do practically, I asked myself, to restore a missing limb or ease his pain?

"I will try to help you," I told him. "I promise."

On the flight home, it occurred to me that I could purchase a prosthesis for Huan so he could begin resuming at least some part of his life.

Back home, while attending Graciela Placak's art class in Tiburon, I met a friend, Jill Kantola, and told her Huan's story, and she generously wrote a check for a new prosthesis for young Huan. I was thrilled and immediately began to plan my return to Vietnam on April 15, 2015, which would coincide with the fortieth anniversary of the end of the Vietnam War. I felt good about doing at least that much, and I continued to wish I could do even more.

Vietnam's Roots of Peace country director, Vo Thi Lien, accompanied me on the drive to Huan's village, and we were surprised to find a large group of people gathered around his home. We watched the group perform a ceremony, something I recognized as a traditional ritual for the soul of someone who has died. Then I saw Huan's mother in the crowd, dressed in white with a bandana across her forehead, a sign of mourning. It was her son the crowd was honoring.

Seeing me from afar, Huan's mother came toward me and, bursting into tears, cried in my arms. We didn't know each other's language, but the language of motherhood was universal. Through a translator, we learned that Huan had died of his wounds forty-nine days before our arrival; he had suffered for nearly four months before finally succumbing to the effects of his burns from the explosion. In Vietnamese tradition, the funeral custom is to honor the dead on the forty-ninth day and create an altar with photos and burn incense. Taking my arm, Huan's mother led me to the altar and gently placed her hand on mine as we both lit candles and wept.

As I bowed my bead, I committed to raising the necessary $20 million by 2020 so we could have a hope of eradicating all landmines in Quảng Tri so that no other children would have to suffer a slow, torturous death because of a remnant of war left behind from long before their innocent souls were born.

Half a world away, in Napa, Thomas Bensel, the managing director at the Culinary Institute of America at Copia, heard this call to action and offered to host the fiftieth anniversary of Earth Day in tribute to our efforts to transform mines to vines in Quảng Tri, announcing, "On the occasion of the fiftieth anniversary of Earth Day, we are proud to celebrate the vision of mines to vines. . . . Together, we join hands with hundreds of California vintners to help restore agricultural lands that were once held hostage to war."

CHAPTER TWELVE

THE CHINA CONNECTION

Therefore, renounce war and proclaim peace
And, seek diligently to turn the hearts of the children
To their fathers and the hearts of the fathers to their children.

—FROM THE CHURCH OF JESUS CHRIST OF LATTER-DAY SAINTS

On December 12, 2017, I attended the Rotary Club of San Francisco's Christmas party. I was reluctant to attend, as I was exhausted from my recent trip to Vietnam, followed by hosting the People's Aid Coordinating Committee (PACCOM) delegation to Washington, DC. Yet we had a tradition of bringing unwrapped toys for children to the event, and San Francisco Fire Department firefighters were there to deliver these gifts during the holidays. My compassion for children led me to drive with bleary eyes across the Golden Gate Bridge.

At the party, a tall, elderly Chinese gentleman adorned with dozens of Rotary medals on his lapel introduced himself to me as Frank Yih, telling me to call him *Yeye* (Chinese for "Grandfather"). He was visiting from the Rotary Club of Shanghai, and wanted to discuss my work with Roots of Peace. We sat together for a long time while I shared my reasons for starting the organization. Frank was fascinated with our McNear family history as well: My great-great-grandfather had hosted over five hundred Chinese families on our property and fostered a thriving business that exported more than three million pounds of dried shrimp to China annually. By the end of the luncheon, I had invited Frank's family to our home.

My husband, Gary, was astounded, as I had not yet begun to Christmas shop for our children and grandchildren. Yet, as always, he was supportive of my intuition. Frank and his wife, Nancy, peered out over our panoramic view and wondered why my family had put their necks out to protect the Chinese families during the Chinese Exclusion Act of 1882. I answered him by inviting their family to join me on a private tour of China Camp State Park, located only five minutes from my home. The Yih family was deeply touched by the tour, as Nancy was born in a province where the Chinese immigrants who had sought refuge on our McNear family property had come from.

Standing on the shores of the beach at the park, *Yeye* announced that he would donate one million Chinese yuan to turn my dream into reality for the children of Quảng Tri. Together, we would approach Rotary International for a matching global grant to leverage my dream to transform mines to vines worldwide.

Just as I had done when Diane Disney Miller had offered a generous six-figure donation to Roots of Peace, I asked, "Who are you?" I could not believe that a stranger would give such a large amount of money.

"I was born in Shanghai and received an advanced education in the UK and USA and have an engineering degree from MIT," Frank told me. "As a young man in the early 1960s, I was hired at Fairchild in the Silicon Valley and was one of the godfathers of the semiconductor, which powers your modern-day cell phone. I continued to pioneer the semiconductor industry in Southeast Asia after making the first integrated circuits in the Silicon Valley. I did well, and then wanted to do good!"

In 2004, Frank founded the HuaQiao Foundation, devoting himself to charitable work helping the poor. "*HuaQiao* combines two Chinese words meaning 'China Bridge,'" he explained. "In China, we deeply respect our ancestors. I am deeply touched by your family's work to respect the land and provide trade opportunities for farmers worldwide. Now, at eighty-five, I will dedicate my life to joining you in planting the roots of peace, and bridging the borders between China and the United States."

I was astounded by his generosity, which transcended borders between China and Vietnam. The humanitarian roots of peace were needed now, more than ever, and the rich history of our McNear family would carry forth into future generations to heal the wounds of war.

A few months later, Frank invited me to China to formally receive a check for $150,000 at a Rotary Club of China meeting in Beijing. While Rotary International is not formally acknowledged in China, the good works of Frank Yih were widely respected.

My grandfather had served as president of San Francisco's Rotary Club chapter in 1940–41, just before the entry of the United States into World War II. Thanks to my family's deep roots in the Rotary organization, Frank invited me to be a keynote speaker before hundreds of Rotarians from over twenty-six clubs in various provinces of

China. My theme was, of course, building the roots of peace by turning mines to vines.

My son Christian had joined the Rotary Club of San Francisco #2, and he also joined me in walking the Great Wall of China. A few weeks later, he joined me on a delegation to the minefields of Quảng Trị. Frank also sent an emissary, Wennie Wen, to see the effects of our work firsthand.

As Christian suited up in his helmet and protective gear and prepared to walk through the minefields of Quảng Trị, my heart began to pound. Here was this precious child, an unexpected gift from God we received after I had survived cancer. His courage and understanding as a young man as he and his parents sacrificed their lives to the minefields of the world were truly extraordinary. Christian had already walked the minefields of the world with me as a child and traveled to Croatia, Israel/ Palestine, and now Vietnam. In another time, a young American man like him would have been walking these fields as a soldier during the Vietnam War. Instead, Christian was taking footsteps for peace.

Christian sacrificed much of his childhood to parents who were deeply committed to making the land safe for other children on the other side of the world. Yet he still developed a sense of compassion that I have rarely seen in other human beings. He is brave, yet humble, and I am incredibly proud of the man he has become.

Handsome and strong, he pulled the visor down over his face and adjusted the protective gear. Then he looked at me, reached out tenderly to grasp my hand, and said, "I'm ready, Mom. Let's walk together!"

CHAPTER THIRTEEN

ECONOMICS OF PEACE IN AFGHANISTAN

Those who hope in the Lord will renew their strength.
They will soar on wings like eagles;
They will run and not grow weary;
They will walk and not be faint.

—ISAIAH 40:31.

The question of whether to give up on carrying forth the Roots of Peace vision after the traumatic Taliban attack on March 28, 2014, was a defining moment. We had listened for four hours to the horror of the attack via a live Skype video, and we all suffered the psychological effects of listening to Mohammad Sharif Osmani describe the youth who had screamed, "*Allah Akbar!*" as he detonated himself in the living room of our Roots of Peace compound. The scene was too much to bear for all of us. For days, I had to walk around the office with a hot water

217

bottle tucked on my chest, as my blood was freezing and I could not overcome the chill in my bones. Gary flew to Dubai to meet with our five employees who had survived, and I had to be strong for our headquarters staff and my family.

Finally, I realized that the entire Kühn family was in a state of shock, and we engaged the professional services of a psychologist to help us overcome our collective grief. I had read that PTSD affects mainly soldiers, but the voices of war had come into the front line of my own backyard. It was a critical moment as to whether we would continue this dangerous journey for peace or cuddle beneath our covers and return to our comfortable lives in Marin County, California.

Many friends were encouraging us to give up. "Enough is enough!" they exclaimed. "You cannot possibly change the norms and cultures of those who have known nothing but war for hundreds of years!" But, again, something deep within my soul told me we needed to carry on. As always, it was a family decision, and when Gary finally returned, he gently held my hand and softly told me, "Sweetheart, we have a moral responsibility to carry forth our mission for the sake of the Afghan families. They've suffered far more than what we endured in just one day of listening to violence and carnage. Together, we must find the strength to carry on."

I was angry. Most of all, I was angry at myself for dragging my entire family into the realm of my naive belief that preserving the principles of peace and love was possible in our world. We were clearly in over our heads, and it would be easier to just give up, be satisfied with what we had accomplished during the past fifteen years, and simply go back home.

Then, our first grandson, Jai Thomas Kühn, was born. Looking into the eyes of our firstborn grandchild, I felt a deep maternal responsibility to protect the innocent footsteps of all children. This healing sense of responsibility washed over me and restored my soul.

With a renewed sense of purpose, we decided to strengthen our Afghan agricultural sector to create jobs and improve livelihoods through our Commercial Horticulture and Agricultural Marketing Program (CHAMP), funded by USAID, and take it to an entirely new level of success since its inception in 2010.

By having faith in Afghan farmers and families, and by not letting the Taliban attack get in our way, we facilitated the export of nearly 90,000 metric tons of fresh and dried fruits and nuts worth an estimated $116 million to international markets including Australia, Bahrain, Canada, Germany, India, Iraq, Kazakhstan, Kuwait, Latvia, the Netherlands, Pakistan, Russia, Saudi Arabia, Turkey, the United Arab Emirates, and the United States.

Over thirty-eight thousand households benefited from our activities, which ranged from demining fields to establishing commercial orchards to exporting high-quality produce. And, by refusing to give up, we helped create nearly nine thousand full-time jobs through opportunities afforded by increased production, quality improvements, and export facilitation. Finally, we helped increase nearly twenty thousand farmers' incomes five-fold by helping them switch from annual crops to perennial horticultural crops. Our Roots of Peace business model earned the reputation for creating the "economics of peace" in a country that is 80 percent dependent on agribusiness.

Roots of Peace was the lead organization to increase exports for Afghanistan. More than five years after the Taliban attack, Roots of Peace helped to increase agricultural exports from $250 million to over $1.4

billion by the end of 2019. These results were astonishing to the international development community.

Roots of Peace also had the innovative idea to bring traders from Afghanistan to visit new markets at the Gulfood exhibition in Dubai, which opened their eyes to a world of trade possibilities. Until then, buyers were hesitant to travel to war-torn areas to purchase fresh fruits. Yet by bringing the traders to new markets, we made business deals possible. During one of our first ventures, funded by USAID, I had the privilege of meeting an entrepreneurial young woman, Kamila Sidiqi, who asked me for my assistance by introducing her to male buyers. Over the next few days, she built up her confidence and eventually ventured out on her own.

Kamila began her company, Naweyan Nawed, to export Afghanistan's dried fruits and nuts, and her business took advantage of the opportunity to build up Afghanistan's promising agricultural sector and to change the country's economic landscape. She has had a remarkable track record of success, and her company employs over seventy-five women and twenty-five men—and she seeks to expand.

"A lot of women are involved in production in Afghanistan," Kamila told me. "My hope is, one day we will have a great environment for our women workers. My aim is not just making money; I think about the workers and the factory too. They are often very poor people, and I want them to have a good life with jobs." Over the years after I met her, her star continued to rise, and she eventually became the deputy chief of staff for Afghan president Ashraf Ghani, as well as the nation's deputy minister for trade affairs.

There are many other success stories in Afghanistan as we continue to train farmers to lead with the shovel and not the sword. In this manner, we are truly turning swords into plowshares by providing farmers with the ability to cultivate their land and provide sustainable peace through exports to new markets.

This would not have been possible if we had chosen to give up hope on our vision to plant the roots of peace, as our program is trusted even in the most remote provinces.

Life is all about trust and collaboration, and that "code of the road" transcends borders with all of humanity.

As word continued to spread regarding our genuine efforts to heal the wounds of war for humanity, more unexpected affirmations appeared along the journey. On the occasion of the 150th anniversary of the birth of Gandhi (October 2, 1869), a mystic from India traveled to meet me to bestow the Mahatma Gandhi Seva Medal from Gandhi Global Family as a tribute to my beliefs, which were in alignment with their founder's beliefs.

Gandhi employed nonviolent resistance to lead a successful campaign for India's independence from British rule, and he in turn inspired movements for civil rights and freedom across the world. He influenced John F. Kennedy, Dr. Martin Luther King Jr., Nelson Mandela, and many others—including me.

As I stood at the podium of the National Gandhi Museum in New Delhi to receive my award while holding the hand of a ten-year-old Afghan girl named Zahra, these words of Gandhi echoed in my mind and summed up my twenty-year journey as a mother: "The day the power of love overrules the love of power, the world will know peace."

My quest for the power of love continues as we seek to eradicate all landmines and truly plant the roots of peace on Earth.

CHAPTER FOURTEEN

FULL CIRCLE

Don't lose faith, and trust that your heart's longing is true.
What you seek is seeking you.

—Rumi

In a journey chock-full of synchronistic, full-circle moments—or coincidences, as many people choose to call them—the following stands out to me.

On May 1, 2019, I took Kyleigh with me to attend an event called Healing Hotels of the World in Algarve, Portugal. The collective energy of the occasion was contagious and uplifting; it was incredibly encouraging to hear the presentations of others devoted to such richly meaningful paths. I spoke of the work being done by Roots of Peace in war-torn lands and of our goals to bring restoration and peace to these people and places that had endured such hardship for so long.

On the first day, after the morning talks, Kyleigh and I were in line for lunch when she struck up a casual conversation with a woman standing near us. Once we'd gotten our food, we split off from the woman and headed to our own table. A few minutes later, she walked over to our table and politely asked to join us.

"I'd like to share something with you," she said. "I am Jasmine, Dodi's sister. My brother passed away that night in the crash with Princess Diana."

A wave of emotion swept through me, and I had to take a steadying breath. A few tears of astonishment were shed. We were all taken aback by the significance of this coincidental connection taking place under the shaded embrace of a lemon tree in Portugal. Princess Diana had inspired me to start Roots of Peace to begin with!

In the summer of 1997, when Jasmine was just sixteen, her family and Diana, Princess of Wales, Prince Harry, and Prince William holidayed together in beautiful Saint-Tropez, in the South of France. One evening, they all went out for dinner in the Place des Lices, where locals gathered to play *boules*, a French game similar to bocce. There were seven or eight of them sitting around a long banquet table eating pizza, and Diana was seated opposite Jasmine.

Diana asked Jasmine what she wanted to do when she grew up, and Jasmine described her desire to be a fashion designer. Diana asked if she had any favorite designers or any favorite dresses Diana had worn, and Jasmine immediately answered that she loved Diana's sapphire-blue off-the-shoulder dress. Diana knew instantly which dress she was referring to, and Jasmine hung on every word as Diana described the couture gown, specifically made for her by the sartorial genius Gianni Versace.

At the end of the holiday, just as Jasmine and her family were about to board the plane home, Jasmine was presented with a big white box containing that very same Versace dress she had described to Diana. Diana's dress became a symbol of inspiration for Jasmine. She was already on the path to becoming a fashion designer, but this gift was a significant talisman of encouragement that boosted her confidence and affirmed her desire to continue that dream. The gesture from Princess Diana was also a demonstration of the grace, generosity, and goodwill that is part of Diana's character and legacy.

Jasmine continued to describe how bittersweet this recollection was for her, because Diana would never witness her becoming a fashion designer. Little did Jasmine know that that summer vacation was the last time she would see the beloved princess or her very own brother, Dodi, alive. Only a few weeks after Diana had given her the dress, they both died, tragically, after that horrific car crash in Paris.

Princess Diana had been my initial inspiration when I began Roots of Peace. I knew from the moment I heard of her work with land-mines that it would also become my cause. I suppose I'd filed the crash in the back of my mind because of how much it saddened me, but it also emboldened me to keep going during the many times when I felt disheartened by one thing or another. Roots of Peace began as a little campaign to carry on the important work initiated by Princess Diana, but it has since grown into a global movement to turn destruction into lucrative and sustainable production. I have her, and a million other peo-ple, to thank for our progress.

The Princess of Wales played a pivotal role in both Jasmine's and my uncannily interwoven origin stories. The meeting with Jasmine under that lemon tree in Portugal affirms a truth I've always had faith in: Things fall into place the right way when you are doing good. Synchronicity, coincidences, *miracles* happen when you're doing the right thing with your mind, body, soul, and resources. I have seen and felt it time and time again.

From launching Roots of Peace with the inspiration of Diana's landmine work to meeting the sister of Diana's companion there in Portugal that day, all seemed to come full circle: lemons to lemonade, hate to love, death to rebirth.

Following that synchronistic encounter, Jasmine kindly offered to donate that sapphire-blue dress to Roots of Peace, in Diana's and Dodi's names, so we could keep turning mines to vines. In a special exhibit at the Leonardo Museum in Salt Lake City, the blue Versace gown is now juxtaposed with the blue HALO Trust flak jacket worn by Diana when she walked the minefields of Angola and Bosnia-Herzegovina.

EPILOGUE

LOOKING BACK

Do not conform to this world,
but be transformed by the renewal of your mind,
that by testing you may discern what is the will of God.

—ROMANS 12:2

Over the past twenty years, people have asked me countless times why my family, my staff, and I voluntarily enter into dangerous places for this cause. How do we live with so much sadness, they ask, so many stories of children maimed or killed? Aren't there less risky ways to try to bring peace to the world?

My answer is always the same: The danger is not landmines. The danger is complacency. The risk is not digging out unexploded ordnance. The risk is failing to dig into our hearts for the strength to join the mission to plant the roots of peace on Earth. We need peace.

What have we achieved over the years? Judging affairs of the heart by their material impact is a cold exercise. How can mere numbers convey the true value of healing broken bodies and souls or restoring someone's dignity with meaningful work and fair pay? Still, some idea of an effort's results is suggested by statistics.

For instance, Roots of Peace began in Afghanistan in 2002. After the Taliban attack on our headquarters, we recovered and helped farmers introduce their goods to markets in India, the United Arab Emirates, Central Asia, and Russia. Afghan agricultural exports grew from $250 million in exported fruit sales in 2014 to more than $1 billion projected by the end of 2019. And with support from USAID, as well as Afghanistan's Ministry of Agriculture, Irrigation, and Livestock and other partners, we are on target to exceed $2 billion by the end of 2020. When we began in Afghanistan, the average farmer earned $800 a year growing low-value crops such as wheat and about $1,200 a year growing poppies for the drug trade. By 2019, the average farmer working in cooperation with Roots of Peace was earning in excess of $5,000 growing high-value crops such as grapes and pomegranates. With the additional income, farming families could afford to send their children to school.

As of this writing, Roots of Peace has planted more than five million fruit trees across all thirty-four provinces of Afghanistan and effectively improved the lives of more than one million farmers and their families. In 2015, we were invited to the palace of Afghanistan's president, Ashraf Ghani, for a private interview with ABC7 News anchor Cheryl Jennings. "We are pleased to report," the president announced to the journalists present, "that the efforts of this one organization, Roots of Peace, have increased the gross domestic product of our nation by a full two percent."

The president's wife, Rula, also expressed her gratitude for our help in improving the lives of thousands of Afghan women, many of whom were now themselves proud farmers, processing dried fruits and nuts for export.

Revenue from Roots of Peace projects—money earned by farmers as a result of our efforts, is nearing $1 billion. In 2018 alone, Afghan traders signed $68 million worth of deals for high-value agricultural products such as apples, apricots, cherries, grapes, melons, nuts, pomegranates, and saffron.

Since its inception in 1997, Roots of Peace has raised awareness and funds to remove well over two hundred thousand landmines and explosive remnants of war in eight countries. Our staff has expanded from a family of six to more than two hundred people, including demining and agricultural experts, financial and administrative staff, and a growing team of government and private-sector advisers.

The growth and impact Roots of Peace has experienced show that with earnest activism, the sky is the limit. In our modern world, I believe it's exciting that the internet and social media provide access to so many social causes. These are forums that can foster a new generation with awareness and compassion if we let them. Charities should not compete, but collaborate. We need to move our thinking beyond silos and into concentric circles of collaboration. When we lift each other up, everyone wins.

The approach we take at Roots of Peace is a holistic one: We seek to restore the value chain by removing landmines, restoring agricultural crops, and providing dignity and hope through continued exports. Our business model for peace moves beyond farm to fork so that farmers can feed their families. When the land is fully reclaimed from the perils of landmines, the farmer not only can feed his family but also has a leg to stand on—figuratively and, in some cases, literally—through the sale of goods once Root of Peace has left the area. Climate change is still a factor, though, as landmines migrate in mud and monsoons and in effect, become virtual. Local citizens may know where the suspected landmines were laid, but when climate and rainfall change, the result more resembles a game of Russian roulette.

It is within our power to remove these deadly landmines from the Earth once and for all. That power is a tangible example of progress in a world that's become jaded in many ways. There are infinite possibilities for grounded peace, but only if we open our minds to global goodness. Humankind may invent deadly seeds of destruction, but we also have the ability to use our minds to create positive solutions to the world's most pressing challenges. It is simply a matter of choice.

Together, may we remove the landmines in our soil, the hatred in our hearts, and the divisive politics in our minds. May we replace them with bountiful seeds of love and heal humanity for generations to come. May we plant the Roots of Peace on Earth.

This is my humble prayer from the heart of a mother.

ACKNOWLEDGMENTS

This book would not have been possible without support from the boy next door. During the 1960s, I grew up near the eucalyptus woods and streams of Dominican College with my neighbor, Raoul Goff. As kids, we played together for long hours and imagined what we wanted to be when we grew up. Our dreams were big—as tall as the eucalyptus trees over our heads. The air was fragrant as we inhaled life. Raoul grew up to become founder and publisher of Insight Editions, and I remain most grateful to him for publishing this book.

It took over a decade to gather the courage to write this book from an authentic spiritual voice while also accounting for the business of peace. A special thank-you to Joshua Greene for giving power to my voice and interpreting my words so carefully. Joshua was an exceptional spiritual guide who picked up the beat in my heart, as he had done before in his acclaimed biography of George Harrison of the Beatles. My thanks to the many others who also helped give birth to this book, including Sam Barry, Dori Bonn, Joan Capurro, Doug Childers, Victoria Cooper, Phil Cousineau, the Reverend Bill Englehart, Sharon Fox, Nannette Griswold, Ursula Hanks, Susie Hoganson, Kathryn Johnson, Ann Laurence, Elaine Petrocelli, Bill Rus, and Kyra Ryan.

I wish to thank my cousins, Nancy, Kathy, and Lynnie Menary (Pelfini), and the many other Glenwood moms who volunteered in the early years to make Roots of Peace a reality, as well as to Frank Doyle of Standingstone, who brought life to my dreams through his artistic talents, and my sisters-in-love Leslie and Grandma Joy for always supporting my dream for peace. My thanks go as well to Grandpa Al, who encouraged my academic dreams when I was attending college to achieve all I could as a woman.

A special thank-you to Dr. Thomas Peters, CEO of the Marin Community Foundation, who incubated Roots of Peace as a 501(c)(3) nonprofit organization in 1997, allowing us to turn our dreams into reality.

Deepest appreciation goes out to Sheila Adams, Maureen "Reenie" Bartee, Sunny Chayes, Alba DeLeon, Suzi Qvistgaard Fransen, Laura O'Malley, George Saribalis, Mary Sinclair, and other selfless friends who would drop in to babysit at the last minute. My children all benefited from your unconditional love.

My deepest gratitude goes to Miljenko "Mike" and Violet Grgich, Erika and Austin Hills, Robert and Margrit Mondavi, and Tor Kenward, and to Diane Disney Miller, whose initial contributions started us in Afghanistan and paved our way for eventually completing thirty-five programs there. To the list I add Joanna Miller, Diane's daughter, who also heard the call to action by Prince Harry at Kensington Palace in 2017 and hosted the twentieth Roots of Peace anniversary at the Walt Disney Family Museum in San Francisco's Presidio. My thanks as well to Bill Murray, founder of the Bank of Marin, and bank president Russ Colombo for their support with lines of credit when we were in a financial low. Together with Joan Capurro, you truly exemplify the Spirit of Marin, along with your loyal staff of extraordinary bankers.

Gratitude also goes to the many Marin County artists who contributed their time, talent, and treasures to Roots of Peace—Dave Jenkins, lead singer of Pablo Cruise, as well as Noah Griffin, Carolyn Jenkins, Jamie Kyle, Michael Pritchard, and George Sumner.

American singer and songwriter Judy Collins not only inspired my generation to take a stance for peace during the 1970s but also contributed her velvet voice to the cause on multiple occasions.

I'd also like to express special appreciation to my dearest friend, Cheryl Jennings, who bravely followed my footsteps through the minefields of three continents. When they asked us our blood type, we both knew the seriousness of the situation. Her news stories catapulted Roots of Peace to international recognition and validated our programs in the field. Cheryl is the real deal, and she is friends with many farmers and landmine victims around the world. Now, as CEO of Cheryl Cam Media, she continues, with her husband, Rick Pettibone, to "walk the talk" with me into the minefields of the world.

Other journalists took intrepid footsteps to cover our story, including Beth Ashley and Frankie Frost, the *Marin Independent Journal*; Jennifer Glasse, Al Jazeera; Kate Kelly, KPIX5 News and the Jefferson Awards; and reporters from VTV4 and the *China Daily News*.

Morton Gothelf, of Morton & Bassett Spices, agreed to buy our Vietnam farmers' black pepper, boosting our program immeasurably. He also purchased saffron from Afghanistan and featured our Roots of Peace logo on every bottle sold in supermarkets. Mort taught me to believe in the value of the extraordinary entrepreneurial gene he calls PDX: passion, determination, and execution. He, too, has earned my gratitude, as has Ron Ivey, senior vice president of Chemonics, who believed in us and championed our initial development projects in Afghanistan. Past

Rotary district governor #5150 Brian McLeran pledged $100,000 for Vietnam when it was not clear we could make our payroll, saving us from leaving a hard-working crew without money to feed their families. He also donated another $100,000 to help us eradicate polio in Afghanistan through our Rotary Club contacts. Our thanks to him.

Thanks as well go to the Rotary Club of China and to Frank Yih, godfather of the semiconductor in the Silicon Valley, who generously contributed one million Chinese yuan for the removal of landmines and the planting of black pepper on former battlefields in Quảng Tri. He is a visionary who transcends borders and connects our world.

A special nod of gratitude to the Tiburon Ladies, a group of powerful "sharks" who were inspired to create a special group of Roots of Peace supporters—Karen Akin, Gail Carlson, Gaby Federal, Alice Flaherty, Jill Kantola, Jan McAbee, Barbara Morrison, Marianne Mullins, Graciela Placak, Karen Plastiras, Mary Jo Schaffer, Lisa Vidergauz, and so many others who produced a spectacular fundraiser at the War Memorial Opera House in San Francisco, where the Charter of the United Nations was signed in 1945. Fellow Marin County supporters Barbara and Charlie Goodman also deserve acknowledgment, as their Shifting Gears team produced a spectacular fundraiser at Checkers with extraordinary chef Stacy Scott. As a Pan Am stewardess during the Vietnam War, Barbara was proud to help heal the wounds of war in Quảng Tri.

My heartfelt gratitude to the many Napa Valley vintners—especially Linda Reiff, CEO of the NVVA, who hosted our initial fundraisers—and, of course, Cakebread, Grgich, Mondavi, Tor Kenward, Wente, Spiriterra, Darioush Khaledi, and the many others that grounded our vision of turning mines to vines. My deepest appreciation goes to Thomas Bensel, managing director of the Culinary Institute of America's California campuses, for hosting the fundraiser for turning mines to vines in Vietnam. And, of course, thanks to the Veterans Home of California in Yountville for planting the Roots of Peace Garden on November 11, 2011.

There are exceptional gentlemen from Marin County who continue to guide me, including the Three Wise Men, Hank Cavalier, Joe Martino, and Ken Tarrant, who join me monthly with prayer and sage business advice. Also, thank you to the Rat Pack at Il Davide—Rick Haenggi, Alan Hoover, Don Leisey, and Jim Placak—for our quarterly meetings and fellowship. And each month, my father, Robert Thomas, gathers with me and his close nonagenarian friends Rich Nave, Leo Andrade, and Tom McGrath to guide me. These are exceptional lunches at San Rafael Joe's or Chalet Basque with the old boys' network!

The late Kofi Annan, secretary-general of the United Nations, and his wife, Nane, supported us multiple times when Roots of Peace was just a dream, and they are always in my prayers. And Gillian Sorensen, former UN assistant secretary-general, graciously hosted me in her New York City apartment overlooking Central Park on numerous occasions. Together, we would sit near her husband's library and ponder, "Ask not what your country can do for you—ask what you can do for your country." She remains a dearest friend.

My thanks also go to Jeff Skoll, who awarded Roots of Peace the Skoll Award for Social Entrepreneurship in 2006 along with a $1 million grant to grow our organization—the catalytic funding needed. Jeff continues to nurture our dreams and our souls with the Wellbeing Project, essential to our continued growth. And thanks go to Paul and Shirley Dean for funding our programs in the fields of Bethlehem and for the many events at their spectacular Spiriterra Vineyards in Napa Valley, where we had a "taste of peace."

To my many loyal executive assistants who worked tireless hours by my side and turned my dreams into reality without question: Allison Bainbridge, Kathy Budzinski, Jeanne-Marie Cresalia, Meg Faibisch, Jennifer Helseth, Lisa Hoye, Laura O'Malley, the roots of peace are firmly planted because of your dedication to my dream.

Our loyal Roots of Peace board members over the years, who oversee the fiscal responsibilities on a quarterly basis, also deserve recognition: Charley Ansbach, Ed Bachand, Diane Baker, Maureen Bartee, Chris Benziger, Dr. Noel Brown, Cecile Chiquette, Joseph Cresalia, Bill Evers, Tor Kenward, Ann Laurence, Kathy Geschke Orciuoli, Dr. Emma Farr Rawlings, Bill Rus, Patricia Sheikh, Scooter Simmons, and Tom Tully.

Jean-Pierre Detry, who badgered me to plant the first cherry trees in Afghanistan, deserves special recognition, as does Dr. Zach Lea, who set the tone and culture for our programs there. Others most worthy of mention include Mohammad Saleem, who worked tirelessly to keep the financial systems together during two stints in Kabul, away from his home in India; Mohammad Sharif Osmani, who served as our county director in Kabul at the time of the Taliban attack; and Cecile Chiquette, who lent us $100,000 when we were in serious debt as a result of insurance owed on our Kabul building after that deadly attack.

My gratitude also goes to Cindy and Bob Sonnenberg, neighbors in Peacock Gap, who had the vision to see the impact of Roots of Peace and nominated me for an award from the Jefferson Awards Foundation, where I ultimately received the Jacqueline Kennedy Onassis

Award. While others may have been too blind to see, the Sonnenbergs stepped forth—and Bob is legally blind.

A special thanks to the talented staff at Insight Editions, who have helped me write this book for nearly two decades: Raoul Goff, my childhood friend, a genius publisher, and a great heart, as well as Rachel Anderson, Courtney Andersson, James Faccinto, Phillip Jones, Vanessa Lopez, and Greg Steffen, for turning vision into reality on each and every page.

I thank my family, friends, and staff around the world for supporting this vision. Thanks also to the special priests in my life—Father Steven Fernandez, Father Paul Fitzgerald, Monsignor Labib Kobti, Father Kevin Longworth, Father Bernard Poggi, and Father Paul Rossi—who bestowed their blessings on our efforts, and to the many interfaith supporters and political leaders who have also shared that vision.

Most of all, I thank my father, Robert Scott Thomas, for instilling the pioneer values of the California West in my soul. His profound belief in my abilities as a woman to achieve my goals was far ahead of his time. In 1972, he inspired my valedictorian speech at Davidson Junior High School, "An Individual in a Mass Society." Thanks to my brother, Bob, who was the family genius in technology and always there to support my dreams. I send my love to my mother, Barbara, a proud teacher, who grew up at San Quentin State Prison and taught me the importance of forgiveness, and to my two extraordinary grandmothers, Lucretia Tufts McNear Thomas and Helen Gleason Rowan Mello.

One particular appreciation of our work bears mentioning, as it brings the story of Roots of Peace full circle. On International Landmine Awareness Day, April 4, 2017, Roots of Peace was invited to Kensington

Palace by MAG and the HALO Trust to meet with His Royal Highness Prince Harry as he expressed his dream for a landmine-free world by 2025. This was significant for many reasons, not least among them the role the prince's mother, Princess Diana, had played in inspiring me to found Roots of Peace more than twenty years earlier.

"My mother had been shocked and appalled by the impact that landmines were having on incredibly vulnerable people," Harry told the press as we stood by his side. "She refused to accept that these destructive weapons should be left where they were. The sooner we are able to clear all remaining landmines, the less chance there is of innocent lives being lost."

Harry then spoke with Kyleigh, who described for him the pennies-for-peace campaign, which by then had collected more than $500,000 to replace minefields with schools and soccer fields. The prince blinked in astonishment.

"I wish there were a thousand young people like you," he said with a smile.

Forever, I will look to God and the heavens to guide me. From my heart, I deeply believe that only the hand of God could have made all this happen. Otherwise, how could a mother and housewife from Marin County turn such an ambitious dream into reality in so many countries? It's a mystery. It's a matter of faith. Each day, I wake up and feel that faith, that one day we may actually succeed in replacing hatred with love, and war with peace.

Each morning, I awaken to my husband, Gary, and his lucid blue eyes encouraging me to be a better human being. My heart belongs as well to the fruits of our love, Brooks, Tucker, Kyleigh, and Christian, and to their children, our beloved grandchildren Jai, Laila, and Amaya, and their spouses, Uppinder, Cassandra, and Ryan, for being the wind beneath my wings.

Like a seed planted in fertile soil, may love take root and blossom around the world. This is my humble prayer.

APPENDIX ONE

KÜHN FAMILY HISTORY

My Granny McNear's home is perched on a Marin County hilltop with a spectacular view of San Francisco Bay. The rolling two-story house sits high enough over the bay that the curvature of the Earth can be seen from the rooftop. Before Granny McNear died in 1994, she bequeathed her beautiful home to me with a written condition: I had to promise to do something for peace. The home is dear to me, and so is the promise I made to her.

The McNear family dates back to generations of seafaring visionaries who voyaged from Scotland to Wiscasset, Maine, in 1701. They helped establish St. Patrick's, the first Catholic church in Newcastle, Maine, where the original John McNear is buried. The McNears worked closely with the Iroquois and Mohawk tribes of New England, the Native Americans who created the Great Law of Peace, which many historians believe inspired concepts embedded in the US Constitution.

From their base in Maine, the McNear family sailed to other American ports. In Boston, McNear relations donated the land for Tufts

University, built in 1852, which opened the first graduate school of international relations in the United States. Another branch of the McNear clan migrated south to Philadelphia. Andrew McNair, a Scottish Mason, was the custodian of the Continental Congress and the official ringer of the Liberty Bell from 1759 to 1776. This was one of the earlier forms of communications in colonial times and a deep inspiration for me as a young reporter for CNN. When the Declaration of Independence was formally announced, Andrew rang the Liberty Bell thirteen times, a gesture of biblical proportions: "Proclaim Liberty throughout the land and unto all the inhabitants thereof."[10] Soon after, an anonymous poet wrote in Andrew's honor:

> *For aloft ring that high steeple*
> *Set the bellman old and gray*
> *He was weary of the tyrant*
> *And, his iron-scripted way . . .*

Years later, when young John Augustus McNear set out from Wiscasset for California in the 1850s, he placed his possessions on the ship but somehow literally missed the boat, which obliged him to travel by horseback through the Isthmus of Panama, through malaria-infested jungles and raging waters. Reaching the Pacific coast, he took a ship christened the *Old Sonora* on an intrepid voyage north. On arrival in San Francisco, he learned that the ship with his belongings had sunk near Tierra del Fuego, at the tip of South America, and he was left relatively penniless. Captain McNear was not deterred, however, and he

---

10. Leviticus 25:10.

eventually purchased thousands of acres in what is now Sonoma and Marin counties.

As the nearby city of San Francisco grew, local farmers could not produce enough food for the growing population. John purchased the cargo ships *Josie* and *Steamer Gold* and began transporting eggs, milk, and butter to San Francisco, and by the late 1860s, he had become one of California's first millionaires. Inspired by his example of perseverance, the McNear family motto ever since has been "Better to light one candle than curse the darkness."

Next, McNear purchased land at Cypress Hill in Petaluma after his first wife, Clara, and their children tragically died in a shipping accident. Today, this is where most of our McNear family ancestors are buried. He became a prominent figure in San Francisco's business, banking, and agricultural circles and was a contemporary of the railroad barons Charles Crocker, Mark Hopkins, Collis Huntington, and Leland Stanford, known as "the Big Four."

The wheat granary McNear and his brother George founded was the largest in the country at that time. This early American McNear also founded the Bank of Sonoma and created the first Sonoma Water Board. With the profits from his businesses, he helped develop both Sonoma and Marin counties, most notably by sponsoring Chinese workers who toiled during the California Gold Rush and built the trans-Pacific railroad to run by his private property of over 2,500 acres along the San Rafael shoreline in Marin County.

McNear stood up against discrimination when the Chinese Exclusion Act of 1882 was enacted and sailed to San Francisco to offer the Chinese refuge on his private land. Eventually, more than five hundred Chinese workers lived on his land, and these industrious immigrants started a thriving business exporting three million pounds of dried shrimp to China each year. The workers were primarily men, so he invited them to send for their wives and establish families. The growing Chinese community in Sonoma and Marin counties greatly respected Captain McNear for his support, and the community grew and expanded into construction and other trades.

My great-grandfather, Erskine Baker (E. B.) McNear, one of John McNear's children, went into the shipping business as well and became a friend to many people, including A. P. Giannini, who owned the Bank of Italy, later renamed the Bank of America. Together, they supported the dream of another visionary, Joseph Strauss, who designed the Golden Gate Bridge. As large landholders in Marin County with interests in transportation, their voices were strong. My father remembers seeing a model of the bridge on his family's dining table in the early 1930s, as the entrepreneurs in the shipping industry envisioned a bridge that would connect two counties across the strong currents at the entrance to San Francisco Bay. This same dining room table of innovation is proudly situated in our home today.

E. B.'s daughter, Lucretia McNear Thomas, and my grandmother on the other side, Helen Gleason Rowan Mello, were strong, pioneering women who were always exemplary in their faith and practices. Helen, born in Mendocino County in 1906, the daughter of a lumber executive, grew up in the redwood forests and rivers of Navarro and Philo. Her husband, Al Rowan, was appointed the first director of education at San Quentin State Prison by President Franklin D. Roosevelt. Al pioneered the notion that prisoners could be educated, and he fostered qualities of forgiveness and redemption among them. Al gave me a sense of positivity and the ambition to become an educated woman myself and to do good in the world.

My other grandmother, Lucretia McNear, was a third-generation Marinite, born on October 17, 1896. She told me she used to sit on her grandfather John McNear's lap and hear him tell tales about "how the West was won," as the epic movie of that name from the early 1960s described it. The McNear family had purchased over 2,500 acres in Marin County that were later sold to Chinn Ho, a land baron from Hawaii.

Granny McNear was the rock of my life. A strong woman of great principle, she instilled courage in my heart that has lasted a lifetime. Quiet and gentle in public, Granny taught me to nurture the power of positive thinking. She believed that God is omnipotent and omnipresent—"omniversal," as she put it. The oldest of four children, she was the only girl. Granny told me stories of riding to San Rafael High School in a horse and buggy on a dirt road, always reaching to make sure her little brothers didn't fall off. She was the big sister I never had, and I was like the young sister she never had.

Granny exemplified love, which I have tried to pass on. She would sit in her garden wearing a straw hat, and birds would gather around her and sing. She was one with nature, long before the expression became popular. I believe she would be proud that I've tried to sow roots of peace from her backyard to lands across the world.

APPENDIX TWO

LANDMINES

It was in 1862, on American soil, that the first modern mechanically fused high-explosive antipersonnel landmine was detonated. A hundred years later, cluster mines, scatter mines, and many other types of unexploded ordnance proliferated in Vietnam, where landmines accounted for 60 percent of all casualties. It was there during the war that the United States' Family of Scatterable Mines (FASCAM) was perfected, allowing retreating armies to spread mines by land and air in seconds.

The Vietnam War became the tragic model for many subsequent guerrilla-style conflicts throughout the world, including the Arab-Israeli wars, which created a demand for landmines. Between 1976 and 1989, Italy alone manufactured and exported $150 million worth of mines. The United States and several European countries profited from their own export of mines, which were cheap to manufacture and quick to deploy. Today, the nations that remain the most affected by landmines are Angola, Afghanistan, Cambodia, Iraq, Israel/Palestine, and Vietnam.

During the late 1980s, governments and nongovernmental organizations (NGOs) began paying attention to the scourge of landmines and their effect on peoples' lives and livelihoods. By the end of the 1980s, the United Nations had launched Operation Salaam, in which foreign military engineers trained 13,000 Afghans in demining practices. By then as well, the International Committee of the Red Cross had begun providing assistance to civilian victims of landmines, and NGOs such as the HALO Trust and the Mines Advisory Group (MAG) in the United Kingdom had started their own programs to remove landmines.

Although the Cold War began to de-escalate in 1989, the Gulf War began in 1990 with heavy defensive mining on the Iraq-Kuwait border. In 1992, MAG began demining northern Iraq. At the close of the first Gulf War in Kuwait, more than five million mines had been cleared by commercial contractors at a cost of $800 million.

In 1995, Belgium became the first country to ban landmines. In 1996, Italy followed suit. Meanwhile, the death count in Vietnam from landmines and unexploded bombs and artillery shells had risen to nearly forty thousand since the end of the conflict there. During the 1990s, an additional twenty thousand civilians, many of them children, were killed or injured by mines worldwide each year.

In 1997, the Anti-Personnel Mine Ban Treaty was signed by many world leaders in Ottawa, but not by the US government. Ten years later, it was unclear how much progress had been made to eradicate landmines. An estimated 160 million mines were still stockpiled in forty-six countries, and Taliban fighters were still using landmines in Afghanistan.

The Middle East remained plagued with mines. As of 2011, three hundred thousand mines remained active in the Jordan Valley, an area prone to floods that carried the mines out of fenced areas to public waterways. That year, US troops withdrew completely from Iraq, which was estimated to contain 25 percent of the world's unexploded landmines. Most of these mines were left behind from the Iran-Iraq War, during which Saddam Hussein's regime planted them by the tens of thousands. There are no existing maps to show where they are located.

In June 2014, the United States at last announced its intention to join an international treaty banning landmines but did not set a time frame.[11] In 2016, President Barack Obama announced a plan by the United States to spend $90 million to remove cluster bombs and other unexploded ordnance in Laos, which he said "is the most heavily bombed nation in history." The United States flew 580,344 bombing missions over Laos, dropping the equivalent of two million tons of ordnance, or 260 million bombs. An estimated 30 percent of the antipersonnel cluster bombs did not detonate.[12] The ICBL research initiative Landmine and Cluster Munition Monitor estimates that the number of casualties from air-dropped explosive devices in Laos since 1964 is 29,000 killed and 21,000 injured. The majority were civilians.

Since its inception in 1997, Roots of Peace has contributed to the removal of more than two hundred thousand mines in Afghanistan, Cambodia, Croatia, the Holy Land, and Vietnam. Sometimes a penny at a time, with the help of Kyleigh Kühn's Children's Penny

---

11. The US Congress had enacted a legal ban on the export of landmines in 1992.

12. Launched from the ground or dropped from the air, cluster munitions consist of containers that open and disperse submunitions over a wide area.

Campaign in American schools, Heidi has raised millions of dollars for the demine-replant-rebuild model she and her husband, Gary, have established through Roots of Peace. Together as a family, they believe in removing landmines from the soil, the soul, and the mind to create fertile ground in which to firmly plant the seeds of love and sustainable peace. The economics of peace is clearly reflected in their business model on various continents.

ABOUT THE AUTHOR

Heidi Kühn is an accomplished social entrepreneur whose work to demine farmlands in conflict zones has brought her international acclaim. A former journalist for CNN and founder of NewsLink International, Kühn covered the *Exxon Valdez* disaster and broke the exclusive story of Andrei Sakharov's death in the former Soviet Union, going on to chronicle the melting of the Iron Curtain and its effect on everyday lives. She brought her gift for framing stories of global importance in the most human of terms to Roots of Peace, the nongovernmental organization she launched in 1997. After proving effective in Croatia, Vietnam, Angola, and Cambodia, Roots of Peace was awarded a $6 million contract by the US Agency for International Development to work in Afghanistan and has successfully carried its work forward ever since, ultimately managing over $100 million in grants from the Asian Development Bank, the European Union, the USAID, the US Department of Defense, and the World Bank. Roots of Peace expanded national exports in Afghanistan from $250 million in 2014 to over $1.4 billion at the end of 2019.

A graduate of the University of California, Berkeley, Kühn studied political economics and has made a career of pushing boundaries and inspiring compassion. In 2002, she received UC Berkeley's prestigious

Alumni of the Year Award for Excellence in Achievement. An accomplished speaker, she is as comfortable with farmers in the developing world as she is with heads of industry and government. In all her work, she has been committed to pure communication, to connecting with her fellow humans, and with common-sense intelligence. Her book is an extension of the gift for which Kühn is best known: winning the hearts and minds of people of different political leanings, national affiliations, religions, and backgrounds.

A fifth-generation Californian whose family was instrumental in building the economy of San Francisco, Heidi is true to her forebears, fearlessly confronting obstacles to peace, and often bucking convention to do so. She draws on her range of experience as a businesswoman, a journalist, and, above all, a mother to scale great heights, calling on all of us to dig deeper in order to build peace in our communities and our world.